PATRICIA CORNELIUS is a founding member of Melbourne Workers Theatre. She's a playwright, novelist and film writer. Patricia has a fierce commitment to class and her work often examines the lives of the marginalised. Her work also includes dramaturgy and mentorship with young or new playwrights. Cornelius is a recipient of numerous awards. She is the recent recipient of the Windham-Campbell Literature Prize and the 2019 Green Room Award for Life Achievement. She has written over 35 plays, including *Shit*, *Big Heart*, *Savages*, *Do Not Go Gentle…*, *Slut*, *Love* and *The Call*. Patricia co-wrote the feature film adaptation *Blessed*, based on the play *Who's Afraid of the Working Class?* She is currently developing a feature film, *Stolen*, with director and co-writer, Catriona McKenzie. Patricia's novel, *My Sister Jill* (Random House), was published in 2002. She is currently working on a major stage commission for the Melbourne Theatre Company.

The ensemble in Platform Youth Theatre's production of SLUT, as part of TENDERNESS, at fortyfivedownstairs in 2008. (Photo: Marg Horwell)

PATRICIA CORNELIUS

LOVELY LOVELY SOMETIMES UGLY

FOUR PLAYS

CURRENCY PRESS
The performing arts publisher

CURRENCY PLAYS

First published in 2019
by Currency Press Pty Ltd,
PO Box 2287, Strawberry Hills, NSW, 2012, Australia
enquiries@currency.com.au
www.currency.com.au

Love originally published in 2006 by Currency Press.

Copyright: *Fierce Love: The Gritty Poetry of Patricia Cornelius* © Richard Watts, 2019; *LOVE* © Patricia Cornelius, 2005, 2019; *SLUT* © Patricia Cornelius, 2008, 2019; *In the Club* © Patricia Cornelius, 2018, 2019; *The House of Bernadette* © Patricia Cornelius, 2019.

The House of Bernadette is adapted by Patricia Cornelius from Federico García Lorca's *The House of Bernada Alba*.

COPYING FOR EDUCATIONAL PURPOSES

The Australian *Copyright Act 1968* (Act) allows a maximum of one chapter or 10% of this book, whichever is the greater, to be copied by any educational institution for its educational purposes provided that that educational institution (or the body that administers it) has given a remuneration notice to Copyright Agency (CA) under the Act.

For details of the CA licence for educational institutions contact CA, 11/66 Goulburn Street, Sydney, NSW, 2000; tel: within Australia 1800 066 844 toll free; outside Australia 61 2 9394 7600; fax: 61 2 9394 7601; email: info@copyright.com.au

COPYING FOR OTHER PURPOSES

Except as permitted under the Act, for example a fair dealing for the purposes of study, research, criticism or review, no part of this book may be reproduced, stored in a retrieval system, or transmitted in any form or by any means without prior written permission. All enquiries should be made to the publisher at the address above.

Any performance or public reading of *LOVE*, *SLUT*, *In the Club* or *The House of Bernadette* is forbidden unless a licence has been received from the author or the author's agent. The purchase of this book in no way gives the purchaser the right to perform the plays in public, whether by means of a staged production or a reading. All applications for public performance should be addressed to The Cameron Creswell Agency/ Cameron's Management, PO Box 848, Surry Hills, NSW 2010, Australia; tel: +61 2 9319 7199; www.cameronsmanagement.com.au

Typeset by Dean Nottle for Currency Press.
Cover design by Alissa Dinallo.

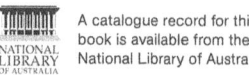

A catalogue record for this book is available from the National Library of Australia

Contents

Fierce Love: The Gritty Poetry of Patricia Cornelius
   Richard Watts   vii

LOVE   1

SLUT   51

IN THE CLUB   77

THE HOUSE OF BERNADETTE   125

Currency Press acknowledges the Traditional Owners of the Country on which we live and work. We pay our respects to all Aboriginal and Torres Strait Islander Elders, past and present.

Fierce Love: The Gritty Poetry of Patricia Cornelius

Richard Watts

The muscular, vernacular poetics that typify the recent works of Australian playwright Patricia Cornelius first appeared in her 2004 Wal Cherry Award-winning play, *Love*; a fresh and urgent take on the *ménage à trois*.

'*Love*, which I wrote about fourteen or fifteen years ago, marks the very first [appearance] of that grungy poeticism that I like to play with. And that's not just being playful because I like the sound of it—though I do—it's also a way of being seductive with a language that is usually too hard on one's ear,' Cornelius told this writer in May 2019.

'The vernacular has a great power—we're frightened of it when people let rip in the tram or the train … it makes us really nervous, because it does express an incredible anger and distain for a world that has done them wrong.

'But to be able to use that language in its real tones … I sort of lucked upon the fun of it, the weird poetic grunge of it, and I think that it's quite seductive. You can seduce people so that they don't walk out [of the theatre] going "I know those people and I can't stand them—listen to the way they speak!" You're kind of a little bit entranced,' Cornelius said.

In her plays about broken souls and bastards, Cornelius works an alchemical magic, transfiguring individuals we might otherwise avoid into figures that fascinate.

Such characters are often volatile, even contemptable, as they spit their fury at the world. But Cornelius writes them with depth and nuance in plays whose foundations are invariably built upon her dramatic bedrock: the socio-political and gender inequalities that shape our contemporary world.

Love was first staged at Wodonga's HotHouse Theatre in 2005 and tells the story of Tanya and Annie, young women who fall hard for each other when they meet in prison. Their relationship is complicated once they're out of jail by the appearance of Annie's other lover, Lorenzo.

It's telling that when Tanya first sets eyes on Annie, the similes she uses to describe her new emotions evoke violence and pain:

> I knew the feeling straight away though I never felt it before, I knew it as if it were a second skin, as if something had crawled up and bit me, like something had fallen off a building site and hit me, I knew, I loved you.

Through her characters' words, Cornelius shows us that these damaged and disenfranchised individuals are so beaten down by the world that they believe themselves unlovable, as Annie articulates:

> The moment I saw you I knew you could love me, I just knew it, that you could really love me and I could love you. Until that second I'd never felt loved, never known it, it was a stranger to me. I thought it was bullshit, a big load of bull, that someone had made it up. Like God. I'd never been loved in my whole fucking life until I met you. And I'd never loved anyone. I didn't think I was capable of it.

Conversely, Lorenzo has a man's arrogance and confidence concerning romance, telling Tanya:

> I know everything there is to know about love.

But as Annie, Tanya and even Lorenzo soon learn, love is a finite resource. Like water, it can easily evaporate, leaving former lovers high and dry—gasping, like fish out of water.

The short play *SLUT* started life as a Platform Youth Theatre production and grew out of interviews and workshops conducted with young people living and studying in Melbourne's northern suburbs. First staged in March 2008 at Melbourne's fortyfivedownstairs (together with *Ugly* by novelist and playwright Christos Tsiolkas as part of *Tenderness*, a double bill) *SLUT* explores the life and perceived crimes of Lolita, a schoolgirl whose sexual confidence both frightens and fascinates her peers.

The play opens with a telling stage direction—*'A chorus of young women sit in judgement'*. It goes on to explore the way women are sexualised and objectified from an early age and how Lolita's peers first admire her for taking control of her sexuality before rejecting her when, in their eyes, she oversteps the mark:

> She was disgusting.
> Over the top.
> She was frightening.
> She was.
> She'd done it with almost everyone.
> Such a slut.

This policing of women's sexuality by women themselves is one of several themes in Cornelius's work connecting *SLUT* with the two most recent plays in this collection: the STCSA production *In the Club* (Cornelius's mainstage debut, which premiered at the Adelaide Festival in February 2018) and *The House of Bernadette* (an adaptation of Lorca's *The House of Bernarda Alba*, staged under that name by the MTC in May 2018).

In the Club explores football culture and women's experiences of it and features an overt and striking scene of slut-shaming set in a nightclub toilet. Two older women, Ruby and Olivia, scold the younger Annie for her perceived shamelessness:

> RUBY: You're overdoing it.
> ANNIE: Overdoing what?
> RUBY: You're pushing it.
> ANNIE: What am I pushing?
> RUBY: You're shoving it down their necks.
> ANNIE: I'm shoving it down their necks. What is it exactly that I'm shoving?
> RUBY: Sex.
> ANNIE: Oh, it's sex I'm pushing and shoving.
> RUBY: It's too much.
> ANNIE: You're right, it's none of your business.
> OLIVIA: I think it's a bit much too.

Set in the West Australian outback, *The House of Bernadette* evokes the Rhinehart family's feuds over mining millions. Matriarch Bernadette, whose second husband Tony has just been buried, 'turns the frustrated rage of her marriage into an uncompromising tyranny over her children … It's a savage portrayal of how women internalise the chains of patriarchy and of the toxicity of sexual repression,' wrote noted critic Alison Croggon in her review at *Witness Performance*.

The target of the slut-shaming here is Rosie, Tony's illegitimate child by an Aboriginal mother. Although she is never seen, Rosie's presence casts a long shadow across the house and its inhabitants, provoking near-hysterical reactions from her half-sisters. As events unfold and closet doors are forced ajar, revealing skeletons and secrets, Bernadette's response is to repress everything—children, truth, everything:

> BERNADETTE: If whatever is going on stays inside, I don't mind.

While Cornelius's poetic rhythms are less overt in *The House of Bernadette* than in other plays, they are still evident, such as in this exchange between sisters Marti and Magda about Marti's friend Victoria, whose husband Gary is violent and controlling:

> MARTI: Won't let her wear what she wants.
> MAGDA: No make-up.
> MARTI: None.
> MAGDA: Not allowed to use the phone.
> MARTI: Not allowed to go out alone.

Victoria's situation recalls Lolita's fate in *SLUT*, which in turn draws on the real-life shooting of part-time model Kara Douglas by her then-boyfriend, bikie Christopher Hudson, in Melbourne in 2007.

In newspaper coverage of the shooting, which saw one man killed and another seriously injured as they tried to stop Hudson's violent attack, Douglas was euphemistically described as a 'party girl', an epithet which stuck in Cornelius's mind as she began to develop the play.

'Christos Tsiolkas and I researched our two separate plays by visiting schools and TAFE colleges with the idea of gender as a starting point,' the playwright told the website Theatrepeople in 2011.

'On the first day of our research we sat in the car and listened to a radio report on the shooting in the city of Melbourne of two men who had come to the aid of a woman being pushed into a car. The woman too was finally shot when she attempted to flee. It was the reporting the next day of her and a friend being described as "party girls" that got my interest.

'In the classrooms young people talked about sluts and girls who came across and weren't worth much and here was one, supposedly a party girl, who actually was shot. I found it deeply sad that the language of hate and sex was still so nasty and stupid. No feminism here and no legacy of the women's movement at all. Still no pleasure, no passion, no sweetness. Sex remains a dangerous game for most girls.'

Just as *SLUT* draws from real life and *The House of Bernadette* recalls a known family, the story arc of *In the Club*'s Annie references the experiences of Kim Duthie, the so-called 'St Kilda Schoolgirl'. After being dumped by the AFL footballer who seduced her when she was just sixteen, Duthie shared nude photographs of his teammates with the world in a memorable act of revenge—an event replayed in Cornelius's play.

In the Club also dramatises the football world's long and shocking history of rape and sexual assault, as well as Cornelius's own complicated response to such crimes.

'I am the first one to admit that when I hear about some young [footballer] and he's got in trouble with some misdemeanour or worse, of a sexual kind, my first response is to feel really sorry for him … and then I have to pull myself up and think, no, fuck you. Fuck you. This is ridiculous. And I think my response is what a lot of people feel; they feel that these young men are absolutely set upon by these "voracious women" and what can they do?' Cornelius said to me in 2018, in an interview for ArtsHub.

'If you just scratch our consciousness a tiny bit we go, "She asked for it". Scratch a little bit more and it's "But what did she expect?" Our language is so condemning and moral about female sexuality. We compliment men who are players—we're the slut and they're the player; we're the whore and they're the stud. The language of it is so fascinating, isn't it?

'And how *angry* we are at them, those women,' she continued.

'I remember at high school, the couple of young girls that were kind of out there—I was fascinated by them. I was so jealous of their freedom but my god, the condemnation that they copped. And even if they weren't actually sexual, but they behaved in a way that was—they had great pluck and used their bodies in a very unselfconscious way. They were terrific. I loved them so much. They were gorgeous,' Cornelius said.

Her fascination for such women endures, with *Love*, *SLUT* and *In the Club*, providing her 'bad girls' with characteristically rich internal lives.

Throughout *SLUT*, Lolita is given a series of monologues exploring her childhood memories—a love of riding her bike fast and feeling the wind in her hair; her sadness and surprise when her father and brothers begin to exclude her from family fishing trips. Such scenes reveal her as a simple young girl who just wants to be liked.

As Lolita ages, her lack of ambition also speaks to the ways in which society teaches young women to curtail their ambitions and their dreams:

> I don't remember a single dream. Not one. I never had one. I never thought, one day I will be something, I will be a famous something or other. I will be a model or ac actress on TV […] I suppose I want to be liked. I want that. I'd like to be liked. That's it. That's all. And … And, I want to want more.

Like the young Lolita, *In the Club*'s Annie—a footy-mad teenager—is initially enamoured of her own strength and speed:

> For the first fifteen years of my life I was a bird in flight, I was a gazelle running across the steppes, I was a cheetah, a leopard, a wild dog. I was agile, swift, lithe, dangerous.

But she knows the world is not kind to girls like her:

> I don't know a single young woman who has kept a childhood dream alive. All their dreams are dead, way dead, died so long ago they barely remember them. Perhaps they never had them.

A dark vein of sexual violence runs throughout all four plays. For *Love*'s Tanya and Annie, sexual assault is so commonplace as to be something they can almost joke about, to be used as a weapon to shock their social worker.

In *SLUT*, Lolita is brutally and shockingly punished for being sexually adventurous and her friends do nothing to intervene. Similarly, the daughters in *The House of Bernadette* gossip about Rosie's sexual exploits without acknowledging the reality of her situation, leaving it for the housekeeper, Penelope, to observe of the gangs of men who fuck her: 'The bastards won't let Rosie alone'.

Nor does *In the Club* shy away from the ugly realities of all too many women's experiences of football culture. The character of Olivia, who tells us early in the play that she is scared of men, is shockingly betrayed

INTRODUCTION

and abused, but Cornelius also provides her a final moment of strength in which Olivia refuses to play the victim.

Similarly, Annie's tenaciousness, her refusal to be boxed in and constrained by her gender, is celebrated in the play's final scene:

> I've joined a team, a footy team, rough as guts, tough, fearless they call us. We are. Wild as can be. I'm recognising more and more of me. Bit by bit. A bit of the old grace, a bit of the speed, the old agility, good hands and something else. Something I never had. The ability to stick, to stay in, to keep grip. Not let go. Like a wild, clawing thing.

In her introduction to *Love*, Cornelius identifies the central theme of her work as 'the story of survival'. *In the Club*'s Annie and Olivia embody that theme—triumphantly.

Melbourne
July 2019

Richard Watts is a Melbourne-based arts writer and broadcaster. He works as the Performing Arts Editor of the arts industry website ArtsHub and hosts the weekly program SmartArts on 3RRR FM. Richard is also Chair of La Mama Theatre's volunteer Committee of Management and currently serves on the independent theatre panel for Melbourne's Green Room Awards.

Carly Sheppard (left) and Tahlee Fereday in the 2019 production of LOVE by fortyfivedownstairs. (Photo: Pier Carthew)

LOVE

LOVE was first produced by HotHouse Theatre at The Butter Factory Theatre, Wodonga, on 27 October 2005 with the following cast:

ANNIE	Peta Brady
LORENZO	Simon Maiden
TANYA	Lisa Sontag

Director, Lauren Taylor
Set Designer, Andrew Lake
Costume Designer, Wiggy Brennan
Lighting Designer, Andrew Lake
Sound Designer, Russell Goldsmith
Fight Director, Felicity Steel

CHARACTERS

>ANNIE, a 19-year-old who can look 40. She is little, waif-like.
>
>TANYA, in her early 20s. She looks and dresses unmistakeably like a man.
>
>LORENZO, no older than 30. A lean man.
>
>The three characters are tough. Life has been hard and unkind and it shows in their eyes and mouths and jaws.

SETTING

>A simple, uncluttered space that is a cell, a room, a footpath.

SCENE ONE

In prison. TANYA *remembers.*

TANYA: The moment I saw you, I reckon, that very second, that's when, I knew it then, I just knew it, I felt it, I knew the feeling straight away though I never felt it before, I knew it as if it was a second skin, as if something had crawled up and bit me, like something had fallen off a building site and hit me, I knew, I loved you.

I saw the bitches smelling you, their eyes slits, tongues circling their lips, mouths filling with spit and I growled at them, I really did, I growled, could've bared me teeth, probably did, because I was that sure that none of them were going to have you, you were all mine and I growled at them, to let them know, back off or I'll let rip. Their hackles rose and I had to square up to them a bit but they scampered off, tails between their legs, they did.

Fell for you then and there. You were wasted and looked like shit, in the clink for a six-month stint, your hair all lank, you had a split lip, you had amazing tits, you were like some bird, yeah a bird, with your wings tangled and I thought, Jesus Christ, you are for me and I'm for you, no doubt, no fucking doubt, I'm going to look after you, nobody but nobody is going to hurt you, not without having to contend with me first, nobody is going to lay a hand on you, never.

You must have felt it. You couldn't have not. It was hot. Wasn't it? I went up to you, knew I had to get to you fast before anyone else got to you, but I couldn't run though I really wanted to but I couldn't run because you wouldn't have wanted me if I'd run, like someone desperate for you. I had to saunter up to you, sure like, and interested, but just so, and I said to you …

    ANNIE *steps forward.*

ANNIE: You are the most beautiful woman in the world.
TANYA: And I had you.
ANNIE: You sure did.
TANYA: I knew it. You were the most beautiful woman I ever had. I couldn't stop looking at you, remember, I'd just look and look at you,

like you were some shining thing and I'd found you and thought if I took my eyes off you I'd lose you and never find you again.

> TANYA *stares at* ANNIE *and* ANNIE *loves it.*

ANNIE: Don't. Don't look at me. Fucking hell, would you stop it, what you looking at anyway, that's what I'd like to know?
TANYA: I'm looking at you, as if you don't know it.
ANNIE: Why? Come on, why? You got a problem or something?
TANYA: I've got a problem alright. Every time I look at you it's as if my heart's going to stop.
ANNIE: Shut up, would you? Sometimes I don't believe you, I really don't.
TANYA: You don't believe me?
ANNIE: No, I don't.
TANYA: Come over here, come on, come over here and you'll believe me.
ANNIE: What?
TANYA: Come on.
ANNIE: Yeah?
TANYA: Come on.
ANNIE: Alright. Yeah what?

> TANYA *kisses* ANNIE.

TANYA: I saw you and it was like …
ANNIE: Like what?
TANYA: Like I told you, like something hit me that's what.

> ANNIE *hits her lightly.*

ANNIE: Like that?
TANYA: Nothing like that.

> ANNIE *hits her a little harder.*

ANNIE: Like that?
TANYA: [*enjoying it*] You couldn't hit hard enough.

> ANNIE *hits her very hard.*

ANNIE: How about that?
TANYA: [*it hurts*] Fucking hell!
ANNIE: Like that was it?

TANYA: No. Harder than that.
ANNIE: Like this then.

> ANNIE *tries to hit* TANYA *again and* TANYA *restrains her.*

TANYA: It was like lightning struck, like getting kicked in the guts, like someone butted me between the eyes, like …
ANNIE: Someone stuffed a cracker up your cunt.
TANYA: You are such a filthy slut!

SCENE TWO

ANNIE: Perfect I reckon.
TANYA: It's not bad.
ANNIE: Perfect. As soon as they see you then they're going to think twice, aren't they? They're going to think, I can't rip her off because her bloke will be on to me. They're going to think, I can't bash her because her bloke will bash me. It's good I reckon, really good.
TANYA: It's not bad.
ANNIE: And it's good because I won't have the money on me. I've always felt bad about that. Who could tell whether they were going to take it back? I had plenty who tried and I didn't fight them for it. It was better to let them have it, better than getting bashed for it.
TANYA: Let them try it and I'll kill the pricks.
ANNIE: Exactly. You'll be there, or nearby, and they're not going to try nothing because they wouldn't dare take you on. I think it's perfect.
TANYA: And there'll be no funny stuff.
ANNIE: This guy I was with, he couldn't give a fuck what they wanted, he was just like them, anything goes, that's what he thought, whatever they wanted I was to let them have it.
TANYA: It'll be whatever you want.
ANNIE: Just head jobs I reckon. It's quicker.
TANYA: We'll clean up. We're a fucking good combination with your looks and my organisation. I'll arrange everything. We'll need a place, somewhere nice, somewhere clean.
ANNIE: In a nice street, a bit classy looking.
TANYA: We might charge more.
ANNIE: Yeah, I reckon.
TANYA: Should charge a packet for what they're getting.

ANNIE: Charge too much and they expect too much. I can't be fucked with any fancy stuff.

TANYA: You don't do anything you don't want to do. You call the shots.

ANNIE: We'll put away a bit every week and get a bit of a stash going and think about the future a bit, just a bit every week, get out of the shit.

TANYA: We'll put away a lot, enough to go away, to … to some bloody where, get a little place or maybe a big place, set something up, something that'll set us up, for life I reckon.

ANNIE: No way am I doing it forever.

TANYA: No way.

ANNIE: No fucking way.

TANYA: No fucking way.

ANNIE: I'm not ending up some used-up slut.

TANYA: Fuck no. That's not going to be you.

ANNIE: Better not be.

TANYA: I can tell you now that's not going to happen.

ANNIE: Better bloody not.

TANYA: It's for a while.

ANNIE: Right.

TANYA: Until we're set up.

ANNIE: Right, until we're set up.

SCENE THREE

ANNIE *stands as if in a trance. She wears undies and a tiny singlet top. She stares out as if at some immense distance.*

ANNIE: [*whispering*] I'm beautiful. I'm fucking beautiful.

    TANYA *wakes.*

TANYA: What are you doing?

    Silence.

What are you doing? Annie? What are you doing? Come back to bed. You're sleep walking again.

ANNIE: No, I'm not, I'm awake.

TANYA: What you doing then? For god's sake, it's freezing, get into bed. You alright?

ANNIE: Yeah, I'm fine.
TANYA: What are you doing out there?
ANNIE: I don't know.

> *She detaches herself from some place inside her head.* TANYA *opens the blanket to take* ANNIE *into bed.*

Hold me, I'm cold.

> TANYA *cups* ANNIE*'s body in hers.* ANNIE *caresses* TANYA.

TANYA: Don't.

> ANNIE *touches* TANYA *again.*

Don't.
ANNIE: I could touch you.
TANYA: Shoosh now.
ANNIE: I'd like to touch you.
TANYA: Don't you worry about me. You let me worry about that.

> ANNIE *attempts to touch* TANYA *again.*

Don't.
ANNIE: Let me. Let me be the one touching. Just once.
TANYA: No, listen, I said don't worry about me. It's okay, alright, just leave it be.
ANNIE: Let me.

> ANNIE *strokes* TANYA.

TANYA: I said, leave it be!

> TANYA *is up out of bed.*

ANNIE: I don't get it.
TANYA: There's nothing to get. I'm not comfortable.
ANNIE: What, with me?
TANYA: It's cramped in that bed, it's too small. First thing we got to do when we get out is get a double bed. A queen-size bed.
ANNIE: You've got great legs.
TANYA: Cut it out, Annie.
ANNIE: You have. You've got legs like a model.
TANYA: Fuck off.
ANNIE: Like dancers' legs, great muscles, they're a great shape your legs. You should show them off.

TANYA: Enough.
ANNIE: I'd show them that's for sure, I'd be bloody putting them on display if I had legs like them. I reckon you're mad hiding them.
TANYA: I'm not hiding them. I'm not doing anything with them, they're legs that's all, they're just fucking legs, so shut the fuck up about them.
ANNIE: Alright. Jesus. Can't I say anything nice? You know that, don't you? That I was being nice about your legs? I was trying to say something nice about you.
TANYA: Well don't.
ANNIE: I like the way you look. Can I say that? Is there anything wrong with that?
TANYA: That's enough, alright?
ANNIE: I haven't said anything. I reckon you're amazing-looking. It turns me on the way you look. You're lovely, well not lovely, you're kind of lovely sort of handsome, like one of those blokes who are pretty, you know what I mean? Like a really pretty looking bloke.
TANYA: Fucking shut up!
ANNIE: Why? What did I say?
TANYA: I told you I don't like it. I told you, didn't I? I don't like it. I don't want you to talk like that. I don't like it. Do you hear me? I don't like it. And I don't want you touching me either. Alright? I don't want you to. I don't like it. That's the end of it. You got that?
ANNIE: Yeah, I guess.
TANYA: Good.

SCENE FOUR

ANNIE *whines.*

ANNIE: I'm not going.
TANYA: You've got no choice.
ANNIE: I'm not going.
TANYA: There's nothing we can do.
ANNIE: What am I going to do?
TANYA: You're going to be fine.
ANNIE: I'm not. I'm fucking not.
TANYA: It'll only be another month and I'll be with you.

ANNIE: I'm waiting for you.
TANYA: You can't wait for me.
ANNIE: You're meant to go first, you're meant to be there to meet me, you're meant to find us a place to live.
TANYA: I know.
ANNIE: You were meant to look after me.
TANYA: A month and I'll be there.
ANNIE: A month's a long time.
TANYA: What do you want me to do?
ANNIE: Stay clean, that's what you said you'd do.
TANYA: Someone's done a switch with my piss.
ANNIE: Yeah right.
TANYA: There was nothing I could do.
ANNIE: Yeah right.
TANYA: What do you think, that I'd put everything at risk?
ANNIE: You did. You couldn't resist.
TANYA: It wasn't my piss.
ANNIE: Yeah yeah.
TANYA: Someone set me up. They did.
ANNIE: You've left me alone.
TANYA: In a month, Annie, I'll be with you.
ANNIE: I don't want to be alone.
TANYA: A month is all.
ANNIE: I don't want to be alone.
TANYA: I know.
ANNIE: I can't be.
TANYA: Sure you can.
ANNIE: You don't understand.
TANYA: I know one thing.
ANNIE: What?
TANYA: I know I love you and I know you love me and that you and me have got something good. One month isn't going to do anything to that. Safe as houses I reckon.
ANNIE: How safe's that?
TANYA: [*whispering*] I found you, don't forget, and I'll find you again and it will be as if I just walked out of this room and came back. We will slip back in that easily, because we fit, when we lie you slip in the

curve of me, we come from somewhere the same, the same shit, we were born in it, we've still got the whiff of it, one month apart isn't going to change that, because we're like the two shells that make up a clam, we close up that damn tight nobody's going to get a wedge between us. You got that?

ANNIE: Yeah, I got it.

While they talk TANYA *dresses* ANNIE.

TANYA: You right?

ANNIE: Yes, I'm right.

TANYA: You sure now?

ANNIE: I'm sure.

TANYA: One month is all.

ANNIE: I'll be waiting for you.

TANYA: Good.

ANNIE: I will.

TANYA: Good.

ANNIE: The moment you put your head out the gate.

TANYA: You'll be the first person I'll see.

ANNIE: I will. I'll be waiting for you, don't you worry.

TANYA: Do I look worried?

ANNIE: And if I'm not I'll be at The George.

TANYA: Okay.

ANNIE: And if I'm not I will be.

TANYA: Okay.

SCENE FIVE

TANYA: Annie.

    ANNIE *screams.*

ANNIE: Oh my god, you're here. You're actually here. I don't believe you're here. How come they let you out early?

TANYA: That'll be the day.

ANNIE: What day is it?

TANYA: It's Thursday.

ANNIE: Thursday. See, they let you out early. It was Friday you were going to be out.

TANYA: Thursday's the day, believe me, I've been counting the days.

ANNIE: Fuck you, I wanted to be there. I wanted you to see me in the parking lot. I was going to have flowers. I was going to dress up, look at me, I look like shit. I wanted to look good for you.
TANYA: You look good to me.
ANNIE: You didn't forget me?
TANYA: No, I didn't forget you. Did you forget me?
ANNIE: No! I was coming tomorrow, I told you, I was going to be there. On the Friday you said, I'm sure you said Friday. And I didn't write, but I can't do that shit, I feel stupid, like what do you say, got a litre of milk at the shop today.
TANYA: Did you get mine?
ANNIE: Yeah, I got them, I tied them up with a blue ribbon and put them in a box under the bed in my room. I never had a letter before. I nearly shit myself when I got the first one. Frank the fucking fat publican handed it to me and I wouldn't take it at first, I thought, fuck, maybe it's something to do with the cops or it's a summons and if I take it I'll be fucked. Then I thought, fuck it's Mum, somehow someone's found me and they're trying to let me know Mum's dead, it's amazing that because I couldn't care less if she was dead, she probably is dead, and I don't even want to know about it, but because of the letter, and because someone wanted me to know, then it gave me a bit of a shock. When I opened it and it was from you I can't tell you how I felt. Like a little baby, all new and smiling and shining, that's how I felt. Frank the fucking fat publican, he thought I'd come into money or something, like I inherited something, or won it, like fat chance, and he starts telling me how much money I owe him. You're here, you're fucking here, I missed you so much. Come on, let's go, I've got a room, it's a hole really but it's a room and we can find something else now you're out.

She suddenly remembers something and tries to cover.

I'll show you the room later on, we don't want to go to the room yet. No, I want you to go back in and I'll come and get you like I said I would. Go on, fucking go back and I'll see you tomorrow with my face looking good and a dress on that will blow you over. Alright, go on, piss off. You're not here. You better fuck off because my love's coming out tomorrow and if you're hanging around me your life will not be worth living. Because my love will snap you in two for just looking at me, my love will tear you apart for standing this close, [*moving closer to* TANYA] my love will snuff you out for putting your lips on mine.

   They kiss.

I've got to tell you something.

TANYA: What?

ANNIE: It's nothing really. If you fucking got out tomorrow when you were supposed to I'd have everything sorted and it'd be all done.

TANYA: What?

ANNIE: We need to get rid of this bloke that's hanging around.

TANYA: What bloke?

ANNIE: He's a dickhead. He's got some ideas about him and me but it's in his head and he won't go away.

TANYA: Where is he?

ANNIE: In the room.

TANYA: You want me to tell him to go away?

ANNIE: Yeah, I reckon he'd get it if it was you who told him.

TANYA: Then I'll tell him.

ANNIE: Oh my god, Tanya, you're here, and everything's going to be so good, so good, so fucking good.

SCENE SIX

TANYA *makes love to* ANNIE.

ANNIE: The moment I saw you I knew you could love me, I just knew it, that you could really love me and I could love you. Until that second I'd never felt loved, never known it, it was a stranger to me. I thought it was bullshit, a big load of bull, that someone had made it up. Like God. I'd never been loved in my whole fucking life until I met you. And I'd never loved anyone. I didn't think I was capable of it. If you love someone you got to do this, and if they love you they've got to do that. I didn't go for it. I thought maybe if I had a kid I might have loved it but probably not. For a while I might but then I reckon I'd stop. I couldn't keep it going. It would piss out. For a while I didn't recognise the feeling I had. I thought it was hope, not love, just hope. Hope that I wasn't on my own, hope there's some other feeling than the crap feelings, hope that life is better than it is. But with you, I feel it alright, it's so tight, nothing can get at it, not even air it's that tight.

SCENE SEVEN

ANNIE *and* TANYA *make a run for it. When they stop* ANNIE *reveals a wallet. She gives it to* TANYA *who pulls a wad of money from it.*

ANNIE: Oh, my god!
TANYA: Jackpot!
ANNIE: He passed out.
TANYA: You're kidding.
ANNIE: I'm not. He went out like a light.
TANYA: Before or after.
ANNIE: Before. Turned around and his snout's up and he's snoring like the pig he is.
TANYA: That's very rude.
ANNIE: That's what I thought.
TANYA: I declare a day of rest.
ANNIE: What'll we do?
TANYA: Anything you want.
ANNIE: Let's eat.
TANYA: For sure.
ANNIE: What you want? Pizza, lasagne, souvlakias, fish and chips, Thai, I like them dips, Indian or Vietnamese?
TANYA: We could have the lot.
ANNIE: Wouldn't mind seeing a film.
TANYA: Why not?
ANNIE: We could go shopping.
TANYA: Definitely.
ANNIE: What'll we buy?

The question is slightly loaded and it hangs there for a moment.

TANYA: Whatever you like.
ANNIE: Um, let me see. Some makeup, and some shampoo. And some clothes, lots of clothes, I'm sick of looking like shit. I need some undies and my bra's clapped out. What else? We could buy a TV. And a DVD and a whole lot of CDs.
TANYA: We could.

ANNIE: What do you want?
TANYA: I don't know.
ANNIE: Could go with some clothes yourself. A new pair of daks. Come on, get something for you.
TANYA: A pair of daks would be good.
ANNIE: Don't you want something else?
TANYA: I wouldn't mind a dog.
ANNIE: A dog?
TANYA: I love dogs.
ANNIE: What kind of dog?
TANYA: A pig dog—they're really faithful.

Silence. ANNIE *looks at* TANYA; *she's got something in mind.*

ANNIE: I know what you'd like.
TANYA: What's that?
ANNIE: You know what.
TANYA: What?
ANNIE: Come on, you know what you'd like.
TANYA: No, I don't.
ANNIE: What would make it just right?
TANYA: Make what just right?
ANNIE: The snuggling up in front of the new TV? What's missing do you reckon?

    TANYA *is silent.*

What's missing?
TANYA: I'm not sure what you mean.
ANNIE: What would make it perfect? Snuggled up all comfy on the couch, got Keanu Reeves on the teeve, got lots of snacks, got your can of beer. What would top it off?
TANYA: You mean …
ANNIE: Yeah, I reckon.
TANYA: I'm not sure if you're thinking what I'm thinking.
ANNIE: I reckon I'm thinking the same.
TANYA: You mean …
ANNIE: That's what I mean.
TANYA: I thought we weren't going to do that.
ANNIE: We don't have to.
TANYA: I just thought we weren't, that's all.

ANNIE: It would go with what we were doing, that's all. We don't have to. It was only a suggestion, that's all.
TANYA: It's a good one I reckon.

SCENE EIGHT

ANNIE *stands alone.*

ANNIE: Tanya! Tanya! Tanya! Put that fucking bastard in jail. Put that weird fucking sick bastard away, not her, not Tanya. He got what was coming to him. Don't put her away. You fucking idiot, she was looking after me!

>ANNIE, *weeping, falls in a heap.* LORENZO *helps her to her feet and dusts her down.*

LORENZO: You okay?

>*He dusts her down some more, concentrating now entirely on her breasts.*

There you are. There you are. That's a bit better now. We'll have you all cleaned up.
ANNIE: Fuck them. Fuck the lot of them.
LORENZO: Hold on, there's a bit more here, hold on a tick, we'll have you right any moment now.
ANNIE: What do you think you're doing?
LORENZO: I don't want you to thank me.
ANNIE: What?
LORENZO: It's a pleasure to help you out.
ANNIE: Stop it. Stop it, would you?
LORENZO: There's just a bit more, not much, nearly through.

>ANNIE *laughs.* LORENZO *stops dusting and smiles at her.*

I'm Lorenzo. Who are you?
ANNIE: Annie.

SCENE NINE

ANNIE *and* LORENZO *fuck.*

LORENZO: Who is she?
ANNIE: Her name's Tanya.

LORENZO: And who is she?
ANNIE: She's a friend.
LORENZO: Oh, yeah.
ANNIE: No, she's more than a friend.
LORENZO: Oh, yeah.
ANNIE: [*gesturing with her fingers*] Me and Tanya, we're like that.
LORENZO: Oh, yeah.
ANNIE: You got me?
LORENZO: Ah …
ANNIE: I love Tanya.
LORENZO: Oh, right.
ANNIE: You know what I'm talking about?
LORENZO: Oh, right.
ANNIE: And nothing's going to come between her and me. And no-*one* is going to come between her and me.
LORENZO: Good on yous.
ANNIE: Got the picture?
LORENZO: Nice and clear.
ANNIE: It's got nothing to do with you and me. Me and Tanya just are. Okay?
LORENZO: Not a problem. In fact I reckon that's great.
ANNIE: You do?
LORENZO: Should be more of it I reckon.
ANNIE: Yeah?
LORENZO: You're you and whatever you do is up to you, you know. You're an individual. No-one can own you. No-one should. Who you love is entirely up to you. It's great I reckon. It's fucking great. We could all love a bit more. The world could learn a thing or two from you, Annie. Get a bigger heart for one thing. Like yours, Annie. You've got a fucking huge heart.
ANNIE: It's true, I've got a lot of love in me. Too much fucking love.
LORENZO: You're right there because you've got this Tanya chick and now there's me.
ANNIE: That's right, there's Tanya and me, and she and I do our thing, and what you and I do is what we do.

He climbs on top of ANNIE.

LORENZO: And what we do is a bit of alright.

SCENE TEN

ANNIE: Tanya never leaves me the way you do.
LORENZO: I don't leave you.
ANNIE: Yes you do.
LORENZO: I'm around the corner, that's not leaving you.
ANNIE: You leave me alone.
LORENZO: I'm using the time well.
ANNIE: You're meant to be there, I could get hurt. Can't you wait?
LORENZO: You're doing your thing and in the meantime I score and then the stuff's there waiting for you.
ANNIE: You score and most of the time I never see any of it.
LORENZO: Really?
ANNIE: Most of the time I don't even see you until you need some more.
LORENZO: Really?
ANNIE: What do you mean, really? Yes, really. Yes, fucking really.
LORENZO: Shit. Are you sure?
ANNIE: Yeah, I'm sure.
LORENZO: I didn't know I did that.
ANNIE: Bullshit.
LORENZO: No really, I didn't know that.
ANNIE: What are you trying to say? That you forget? Bullshit you forget.
LORENZO: No, I'm telling you, I didn't know. I didn't know I did that. And I'm not going to do it again.
ANNIE: Until the next time.
LORENZO: I didn't know I was being an arsehole. And I don't want to be. That's the last thing I want, is to be an arsehole, because you're everything to me.
ANNIE: Bullshit I'm everything to you.
LORENZO: That's where you're wrong, you are, you're my woman and I've been a dickhead and I'm not going to be a dickhead anymore.
ANNIE: I'm not your woman, I'm your bank teller, I'm your source of cash, I'm your bloody ATM machine.
LORENZO: I've been an arsehole, and a dickhead, and a bastard, but I never think of you like that. You are my woman and money's got nothing to do with that. If you couldn't work, if you didn't have a cent, what you think? You think I'd dump you?

ANNIE: Yeah, you probably would.

LORENZO: Arsehole, dickhead, bastard, fucking prick, I'm all those things if you think I'd do that.

ANNIE: And the rest.

LORENZO: I'm turning over a new leaf. I'm not going to leave you, I'm not going to score until you say so, I'm not going to take advantage of you because I think we've got something pretty special and I don't want to fuck that up.

ANNIE: Something pretty special?

LORENZO: Yeah, something pretty bloody special.

ANNIE: What? What have we got?

LORENZO: We've got something pretty good I reckon. Something really good.

ANNIE: Is that it? Is that all you can say about it?

LORENZO: What do you want me to say?

ANNIE: I want you to say more than that.

LORENZO: Alright. I think we're onto something, you and me, something … good, something special, something bloody beautiful.

ANNIE: Fucking hell, Lorenzo, ever heard of love, of saying I love you, ever heard of that?

LORENZO: Yeah, of course, and that, I love you, I didn't say that because I thought you'd know that and I was trying to say something better than that.

ANNIE: There is nothing better than that.

LORENZO: Alright. I love you, Annie, I love you, I really do love you, I love you, I love you, I love you, I love you.

ANNIE: Alright already.

LORENZO: Annie?

ANNIE: What?

LORENZO: I love you.

ANNIE: Enough.

LORENZO: Just one more thing. No, just one last thing.

ANNIE: What?

LORENZO: I love you.

> ANNIE *screams and playfully goes for* LORENZO. *He cups her in his arms.*

I'm not stuffing this up. I've had so many stuff-ups and I don't mind telling you it's me who stuffs it, but I've had it with the stuff-ups. I want it to work, I want us to be good, I want us to hang in there, through thick and thin. I want us to last the distance, to be there for each other, you know what I mean. Like serious, for once in my life be serious about love and what that entails, what you give up, what you let go, stop thinking about yourself the entire fucking time. I'm looking forward to that, to thinking about someone else for a change, thinking about how they feel, how they're going. I'm ready for it. I want to take it on. You and me, loving each other, I reckon it's going to be great. You with me?

ANNIE: Lenny, you're gorgeous, you know that?

SCENE ELEVEN

ANNIE *is on the phone.* LORENZO *has his arms around her, kissing and nuzzling her while she talks.*

ANNIE: He's mad.

LORENZO *acts mad.*

Very mad. He's really funny. Most of the time, he's really funny. Yeah of course, yeah of course, alright I'll tell him. [*To* LORENZO] Tanya says if you're not good to me she'll kill you when she gets out.

LORENZO *shrieks in feigned terror.*

Did you hear that? He's shitting himself. No, no he's really good. He really is. He does all that. Yeah, he does that. Yeah of course he does. He's done that once. Once. He won't do it again. He was really sorry. He won't do it again, he promised. [*To* LORENZO] She wants to talk to you.

LORENZO *pulls a face of mock terror.* ANNIE *hands him the phone.*

LORENZO: Hi, Tanya. Hi. Yeah, gooday.

Pause.

Fuck no, that was bad, that won't happen again, that was bad. I didn't understand, I didn't know how important it was. It was only the once.

ANNIE *whispers mischievously over his shoulder and he quickly covers the receiver.*

ANNIE: Yeah right.
LORENZO: I don't leave her now.
ANNIE: You leave me all the time.
LORENZO: What? I don't know what she's saying. It won't happen again, Tanya. It was a dumb move. I'd never leave her like that again.
ANNIE: Liar.
LORENZO: I respect her too much.
ANNIE: Fucking liar.
LORENZO: It kills me I put her in danger.
ANNIE: You are so full of it.
LORENZO: Okay, here she is, I'll put her back on. What?

He rolls his eyes.

Yeah, yeah, I know. Yeah, I've heard the stories. She'll be fine. Here.

ANNIE *takes the phone.*

ANNIE: Yeah, it's me. I can't wait for you to meet him, you'll like him. He's a bastard though. Don't worry I can handle him. Yes I can.

She turns away and speaks more intimately into the phone.

You don't mind, Tan, do you? You don't mind. You know how it is. I freak out without you, you know that, don't you? He's filling in until you come home. Then we'll be back on track and start thinking about the future. No, he's gone.

She gestures for LORENZO *to be quiet.*

Yeah, he's gone. We can talk. Yeah, we can. Hi. Hi. Hi. Me too. Me too. Yeah, me too. So much. So much. So fucking much. Love you. Love you. Yes really. Yes, of course I do. Love you. 'Bye. Love you. 'Bye. 'Bye. 'Bye.

SCENE TWELVE

TANYA *and* LORENZO *turn to one another.* LORENZO *is momentarily shocked at* TANYA*'s appearance. In silence they settle in and eye each other off for a long time.*

ANNIE: So you two, this is you Tanya, and this is you Lorenzo, you can call him Lennie, Tanya, I do. So here we are, and we've got this room. Have we, Lennie, did you pay the rent on this room? Anyway

I think we've got this room and its okay, we'll make it work, until we get something bigger of course. So, this is good, I reckon it's good because I've got you both and it's only a matter of time before you get to know each other and you'll feel like I do. Don't you reckon? We'll see how it goes because fucking hell I don't care how it usually goes, I couldn't give a fuck, because how it usually goes is usually shit, and we can do whatever we want, whatever we think is a going thing.

TANYA: [*to* LORENZO] I'll take care of the business side of things.

    Pause.

LORENZO: Sure thing, sure, sure, that's not my thing, you're right, absolutely right, okay good.

TANYA: Annie, you'll need to fill me in.

ANNIE: Not now. Come on, this is great, you're out, Tanya, and we're all here, the three of us. For the first time I've got my loves together. We've got to do something to celebrate, got to do something nice together, so you two can get to know each other. Where we go? What'll we do? Let's go and get drunk. Do something great. Celebrate. Make an occasion of it. I'm sick of doing nothing.

LORENZO: I'll handle the money.

TANYA: I don't think so.

LORENZO: I think so.

    Pause.

Sure. Sure. Whatever you think's right.

ANNIE: We could go somewhere. Somewhere we've never been, somewhere different, I don't know, somewhere where we can look at things that we've never seen before, strange things, different things, something different would be good.

LORENZO: I'll take care of everything else then, Tanya.

TANYA: No worries. That's good.

ANNIE: I don't know how long it's been since I've done something different, I haven't been nowhere, I don't reckon ever, I've not seen anything, I'm kind of dying for a change, dying for it. I'm not letting this chance go, we're together for the first time and we've got to do something with that, or else, I don't know, we're just going to let it piss out.

LORENZO: If there's anything you want me to do, just ask, alright, because I'm here. I'm not going anywhere. I might as well be doing something. Actually I should be doing something, you know, to earn my keep. I'm not a hanger-on kind of bloke, not a shag on some rock, so you know, just think about it, and let me know what I can do because I'll do it, no worries, just got to ask.
ANNIE: I can't think of any place.
TANYA: There's stuff for you to do.
LORENZO: Yeah, good. Like what?
TANYA: There's something.
LORENZO: Of course, there'd be plenty I reckon.
TANYA: Just got to think about it.
LORENZO: Like I said, I'm not going anywhere, so might as well be doing something
TANYA: There is something you can do.
LORENZO: Yeah, what's that?
TANYA: You keep Annie happy. How about that?
LORENZO: Goes without saying, mate, goes without saying. That's not asking anything, that's what I'm here for, first and foremost, to keep my girl happy.
TANYA: You can do that?
LORENZO: Sure thing. Isn't that right, Annie?
ANNIE: What?
TANYA: He can make you happy?
ANNIE: He can do that.
TANYA: That's settled then.
LORENZO: Seems pretty good to me.
ANNIE: Take us somewhere then. That'd make me happy.
LORENZO: Anywhere you like, my darling.
ANNIE: Take us somewhere different, to something new.
LORENZO: Name the place.
ANNIE: Where something's going on, where we can look at something.
LORENZO: The pictures.
ANNIE: Not the pictures, I've been to the pictures.
LORENZO: Luna Park, you like it there.
ANNIE: Not Luna Park, I've been there tons of times.
LORENZO: Jesus, Annie, I don't know.
ANNIE: Think of somewhere.

LORENZO: Could go to the arcade.

ANNIE: Not that. I don't want to watch you for fucking hours shooting aliens.

LORENZO: What then?

ANNIE: I don't know. I want to look at something, see something I've never seen.

LORENZO: Jesus, Annie, I don't know what you want. Do you want me to take you to the fucking museum or something?

ANNIE: Why not!? I've never been.

TANYA: The museum's closed at night.

ANNIE: Oh, shit!

LORENZO: And we've got a small problem.

ANNIE: What?

LORENZO: We're short of cash.

ANNIE: No we're not.

LORENZO: We're flat chat.

ANNIE: I've got some money.

LORENZO: No you haven't.

ANNIE: Do you think I'm stupid? I put some under the mat.

LORENZO: I had to use that.

ANNIE: Fucking hell, Lennie. Luckily I've got some stashed behind the mirror.

LORENZO: Found that.

ANNIE: What!?

LORENZO: Took that.

ANNIE: Fucking hell, Lennie. Tanya, thank god you're back. Now we can't do anything, Lennie, you realise that?

LORENZO: Sure we can. It's early. We can go somewhere nice later on, go dancing. How about that?

ANNIE: What with? How we going to do that?

TANYA: Reckon you could work for a couple of hours?

ANNIE: Now?

TANYA: I don't see we've got much choice.

ANNIE: I wanted us to do something together.

LORENZO: We will, we'll get some cash first and then we'll do something.

ANNIE: Fuck you, Lenny. Fuck you!

LORENZO: Come on, baby, don't be like that.

SCENE THIRTEEN

ANNIE *is somewhere deep and far away.*

ANNIE: I'm beautiful. I'm fucking beautiful.

    LORENZO *calls from the other side of the door.*

LORENZO: Annie!
ANNIE: [*quietly*] Leave me alone. Would you? Leave me alone for a moment at least.
LORENZO: Annie.
ANNIE: What?
LORENZO: Annie.
ANNIE: What? What the fuck do you want?
LORENZO: Open the door.
ANNIE: No.
LORENZO: Come on, Annie, open the door.
ANNIE: Leave me alone, Lenny, would you?
LORENZO: Annie. Open the door, for a moment, come on, let me in.
ANNIE: Why?
LORENZO: I want to talk to you.
ANNIE: What about?
LORENZO: Come on, please, open the door.
ANNIE: What do you want?
LORENZO: I'm strung out.
ANNIE: Leave me alone.
LORENZO: I'm strung out bad, Annie.
ANNIE: Where's Tanya?
LORENZO: She told me to talk to you.
ANNIE: She did not.
LORENZO: She told me to tell you that you have to look after me.
ANNIE: She did not.
LORENZO: She told me to tell you that you better look after her man.
ANNIE: Her man!
LORENZO: Yeah. I'm her man, that's what she said, and you've got to look after me.
ANNIE: You're not Tanya's man.

LORENZO: If I'm your man then I'm Tanya's as well, that's what she said. And she said you have to look after me.
ANNIE: That would make you just about gay, Lorenzo, and somehow I don't think so.
LORENZO: Come on, Annie baby, please.

    ANNIE *pushes past* LORENZO.

Don't wake Tanya, baby. I'll leave you alone, alright, I just wanted to talk, just you and me, for a change, just us two.
ANNIE: Leave me alone, Lenny.
LORENZO: Look, I've left you. I don't want anything. Just talking, that's all.
ANNIE: Don't ask me.
LORENZO: What? I'm not asking. Not a thing.
ANNIE: You've got to stop.
LORENZO: What am I doing? I'm not doing nothing, nothing, not asking, nothing.
ANNIE: Go away.
LORENZO: Where to? I'll go. You tell me and I'll go.
ANNIE: Just go away.
LORENZO: I'm going.
ANNIE: Go on then.
LORENZO: Can't I say goodbye?
ANNIE: Goodbye.
LORENZO: Not a kiss, not a hug, nothing at all?

    ANNIE *kisses* LORENZO *and he holds her in his arms.*

I'm so strung out, baby.
ANNIE: Let me go.
LORENZO: I'm just so strung out.
ANNIE: Let me go, Lennie.
LORENZO: Come on, Annie, help me, help me out.
ANNIE: No. No. Tanya!
LORENZO: Don't wake her.
ANNIE: Tanya!
LORENZO: Fuck you, I said don't wake her.
TANYA: What?
ANNIE: He's driving me crazy again.

TANYA: Fuck off, Lenny, leave her alone.
ANNIE: He won't let me go.
TANYA: Let her go.
ANNIE: He won't let me.
LORENZO: Come on, baby, help me.
TANYA: [*more serious*] Let her go, Lenny.
ANNIE: You just had some.
LORENZO: I need more, Annie. I need more.
ANNIE: Let me go.
TANYA: [*getting up*] Let her go, Lenny.
LORENZO: I need more.
TANYA: How come you need more?
ANNIE: You stick a ton of it up your arm and you still need it, it's too much.
LORENZO: I'm bigger than yous, I need more.
TANYA: You're greedy. You don't need it, you just want it.
LORENZO: You're right, you're right, and I tell you what, tomorrow I'm cleaning up. No shit. I've had it with shit. Tomorrow, shit and me, we're through. So come on, Annie.
TANYA: Leave her, Lenny.
LORENZO: You go back to sleep, Tanya, I'll take Annie out, just a few tricks, baby, I'll be with you.
ANNIE: No. Leave me alone.
TANYA: You should be dead with the amount you suck up.
ANNIE: How come you're not dead?
TANYA: Should be.
ANNIE: You've had enough to kill a fucking bull.

> LORENZO *falls to his hands and knees and snorts and paws the ground. He charges* ANNIE *and chases her around the room. It is a gorgeous performance and* TANYA *and* ANNIE *warm to it. He begins to chase* TANYA *too and both women shriek with delight at the game.* TANYA *becomes the matador and* ANNIE, *the beautiful senorita. Finally* TANYA *spears the bull and he dies.*

LORENZO: Annie. Annie. Annie.
ANNIE: Fucking hell.
LORENZO: Annie. Annie. Annie.

ANNIE *and* TANYA *look at each other.* TANYA *shrugs her shoulders and* ANNIE *sighs deeply.*

ANNIE: Alright. Alright, I'm going.

Immediately LORENZO *puts his head up.*

LORENZO: Love you, baby, love you.

SCENE FOURTEEN

ANNIE, LORENZO *and* TANYA *sit on the edge of the bed facing the wall. At intervals each of them falls back onto the bed, their heads hanging over the edge.*

LORENZO: Love it.

Pause.

Love it.

Pause.

Nothing like it.

Pause.

Nothing.

Pause.

Love it.

SCENE FIFTEEN

ANNIE *is asleep.* TANYA *and* LORENZO *sit up either side of her. Silence.*

TANYA: Why don't you fuck off, Lorenzo?
LORENZO: Because I'm in love, mate. I'm in love.
TANYA: What do you know about love?
LORENZO: I know everything there is to know about love.
TANYA: When I love somebody I give everything I've got.
LORENZO: That's me.
TANYA: I'm there one hundred percent.
LORENZO: Ditto.
TANYA: There's no stopping me, I am that devoted.
LORENZO: And again.

TANYA: I'm in there, totally.
LORENZO: And again.
TANYA: Bullshit. When I love, I love.
LORENZO: You reckon you love better than I love?
TANYA: You can test me. I stay in there, I never falter, not for a second. When I've got my woman, that's it, she's everything to me. I don't look around, I don't fuck around, I don't feel it for anyone but her.
LORENZO: That's me. Exactly.
TANYA: And I take the shit. There's always shit in love.
LORENZO: I've never been with a woman that isn't full of shit.
TANYA: It's their hormones and their periods and all that crap. It drives them nuts.
LORENZO: They're always wanting something, needing more.
TANYA: That's the way they are. I accept that.
LORENZO: I think, fuck, how much more do they want? They're that empty, worse than a junkie dying for a hit. They're a bottomless pit. It's like they've got no core, no backbone.
TANYA: There's nothing you can do except give them as much as you can give.
LORENZO: That's it.
TANYA: I give lots when I'm in love, I give a ton.
LORENZO: I'm always giving out.
TANYA: And with all the shit, and the whingeing, and the cranky period crap, and never being happy no matter what, my love never wavers. I'm there.
LORENZO: Me too. Me too.
TANYA: I'm not into this macho shit. I don't go for the backhander or for putting them down. I never throw my weight around.
LORENZO: [*less certain*] No way.
TANYA: Yeah, right.
LORENZO: No way!
TANYA: I'm good to my woman. I like to take her out and show her around. I like to be with her, spend time with her, I like to make her laugh, and I like it when her back arches when I put my fingers …

She realises she has said too much. LORENZO *smiles at her omission. They laugh briefly.*

I know how to love.

SCENE SIXTEEN

TANYA *and* LORENZO *call to* ANNIE *who has locked herself away.*

TANYA: Annie, Annie, Annie, what's wrong? Come on. Come out. I'll put you to bed. You haven't slept. I'll rub your back, how about that? Would you like that? Annie?
LORENZO: Annie, Annie, Annie, come on out, baby. What you doing in there? I miss you, Annie, I miss you bad. Did you hear me? I miss you. Annie?
TANYA: Annie, Annie, Annie, you got to answer me. You're not doing something stupid in there, are you?
LORENZO: Annie, Annie, Annie, you got some stuff in there? Have you?
TANYA: Annie.
LORENZO: Annie.
TANYA: We've been talking, Annie. We think you've been working too hard.
LORENZO: Way too hard.
TANYA: You need a holiday.
LORENZO: And that's just what you're going to get.
TANYA: What do you think of that?
LORENZO: We all need a holiday.
TANYA: A real holiday, like at the beach.
LORENZO: On an island, one of them tropical islands.
TANYA: Or you can lounge around here, just take it easy, do nothing, absolutely nothing. How about that?
LORENZO: How about that, baby?
TANYA: You deserve it.
LORENZO: You sure do.
TANYA: What do you think?
LORENZO: Annie? Hey, baby? [*To* TANYA] This is giving me the shits.
TANYA: She'll come out soon.
LORENZO: Fucking slut, what she fucking want?
TANYA: Shut up. Tell her you love her.
LORENZO: Fuck her.
TANYA: Just tell her.
LORENZO: You tell her.

TANYA: She knows I love her.
LORENZO: Tell her again.
TANYA: She wants to hear it from you.
LORENZO: Love you, baby. You know that, don't you? Love you.
TANYA: Put a bit of feeling into it, would you?
LORENZO: Hey, baby, you know it's hard when you do this. I fall apart without you. Just seeing you, baby, means everything to me. Holding you, feeling you... [*To* TANYA] You fuck off then, this is embarrassing.

He lowers his mouth to the keyhole. TANYA *retreats.*

Listen, Annie, baby, baby. Listen. I asked Tanya to give me a minute, to talk, just you and me, baby. You hear me, baby? This is something, I reckon, you and me, and Tanya. But you and me, I mean we've got a pretty powerful love, like it's sometimes out of control, like it's going to take off sometimes, but in the end, Annie, it's just meant to be.

LORENZO *continues, but in a whisper.*

TANYA: Come on. Come on. Fuck you, Annie. Fuck you. Get it to-fucking-gether.

ANNIE *emerges, shrieking with excitement.*

ANNIE: Do you know what?
TANYA: What?
ANNIE: I am the happiest woman in the world.
TANYA: Good.
ANNIE: Do you know why?
TANYA: Why?
ANNIE: Lenny's asked me to marry him. We're going to get married. Can you believe it?

Pause.

Tell her.

LORENZO: It's true. Annie has accepted my hand in marriage.
ANNIE: Isn't it wonderful? Are you happy for me?

Pause.

I'm happy for me. I want you to be happy for me. No-one's ever asked me to marry them before.

TANYA *remains silent.*

Come on, be happy for me. Tanya? Aren't you happy for me?

TANYA: Where do I go?
ANNIE: What? Oh, my darling, you're there.
TANYA: Where?
ANNIE: You're with me, always, forever.
TANYA: How's that?
ANNIE: Nothing's going to change between you and me.
TANYA: I don't know where I am.
ANNIE: You are so gorgeous, Tanya. Nothing's going to change. Believe me. I love you. Nothing's going come between us. Nothing could.
LORENZO: Doesn't change a thing, Tanya.
ANNIE: Not a thing.
TANYA: Better not.
ANNIE: You know better than that, Tan.
LORENZO: And I was thinking, I'd like you to be my best man.

There's a pause and then TANYA *and* ANNIE *and* LORENZO *laugh uproariously.*

ANNIE: This is the happiest day of my life.

She busily picks up items of clothing, looking for various garments and then dressing in them.

I'm going to wear white and fuck anyone who thinks I shouldn't because it's my wedding and I've always wanted to wear a white bridal gown.

ANNIE *sweeps up her hair.*

TANYA: What are you doing?
ANNIE: What?
TANYA: What are you doing?
ANNIE: Getting ready for work of course.

TANYA *and* LORENZO *look at one another and smile.*

SCENE SEVENTEEN

TANYA *and* LORENZO *are alone.*

LORENZO: I've been thinking, Tanya.
TANYA: Yeah, really?
LORENZO: Yeah, I've been thinking about me and Annie.

TANYA: Yeah, really.
LORENZO: I've been thinking that maybe Annie and I need some time on our own.
TANYA: You were thinking that, were you?
LORENZO: Take some time to kind of think about our future.
TANYA: What's there to think about?
LORENZO: Got to consider what we do, me and Annie.
TANYA: What you do?
LORENZO: Now we're going to make a commitment to each other.
TANYA: What are you talking about?
LORENZO: Me and Annie that's what, making a commitment.
TANYA: You're not going to marry Annie.
LORENZO: I asked her, didn't I?
TANYA: Yeah, you *asked* her.
LORENZO: And she said yes.
TANYA: So what?
LORENZO: And she was excited about it, don't you remember?
TANYA: So what?
LORENZO: It's as simple as this, Tan, I've got something you haven't got.

Pause.

TANYA: A dick!?
LORENZO: I've got a dick and that's a lot.
TANYA: What?
LORENZO: Being a man, that's what I've got.
TANYA: Big fucking deal.
LORENZO: I know. It's crap but that's the way it is. Nothing to do with me. It means more, that's all.
TANYA: Who says?
LORENZO: The world.
TANYA: I don't give a shit what the world says.
LORENZO: And that's what Annie says.
TANYA: She doesn't say that.
LORENZO: She doesn't say it, but that's what she thinks because that's what the world thinks.
TANYA: I don't give a shit what the world thinks.
LORENZO: You and I don't give a shit, we don't give a shit, but the world does. And so does Annie. It's hard for you, Tanya, I can see that

because as far as the world goes you don't fit, you know. What are you, you know? You don't know what you are. I don't know what you are. You know what I mean?

TANYA: I know what I am.

LORENZO: Yeah, but what's the world make of you? They don't know how to figure you out. I don't know how to figure you out. How in hell's the world going to?

TANYA: Fuck the world.

LORENZO: They're not going to try to figure me out because they don't have to because I'm a man, that simple, and so I just am, that's all. Whereas you … you're a fucking enigma, mate.

TANYA: I don't have to explain myself.

LORENZO: Course you don't. There's nothing you could say anyway, to the world, there's nothing because they wouldn't get it, they don't want to get it. You freak them out.

TANYA: Fuck off!

LORENZO: You can't blame them, Tan. Look at you. You confuse them. You look like a man, you act like a man, you could be a man but you're not.

TANYA: I said, fuck off.

LORENZO: And you're not a woman either. Well, you are but you're not.

TANYA grabs LORENZO by the shirt front and pulls him hard into her face.

TANYA: I'm not a man, Lenny. I'm better than a man. Got that? Better.

They are still, face to face, tensed up like a couple of snakes. Finally TANYA relaxes and LORENZO follows. They continue to stare. It is indiscernible who initiates but they slowly move in closer and it becomes so close they kiss. At first LORENZO kisses TANYA hard, but soon TANYA takes over, kissing him passionately and aggressively, and he responds. Suddenly they stop. They step back and look at each other. LORENZO is first to break the hold and once their eyes are unlocked neither can look at one another.

LORENZO: Fuck me. Fuck me. What was that?

TANYA: You liked that, did you?

LORENZO: Fuck me, what was it?

TANYA: You liked it.

LORENZO: It was wild.
TANYA: Annie likes it too. She likes it a lot.

SCENE EIGHTEEN

ANNIE, TANYA *and* LORENZO *sit close but apart.*

ANNIE: I'm cold.
> *Pause.*

I'm cold.
> *Pause.*

I'm fucking cold!
LORENZO: We heard you.
TANYA: We thought you'd like it.
ANNIE: What's to like?
LORENZO: We thought you wanted to do something.
TANYA: To go somewhere.
ANNIE: To the beach!
LORENZO: We thought you'd like to get out.
ANNIE: It's fucking winter!
TANYA: Christ, Annie.
LORENZO: It's something different.
TANYA: You've been going on and on about doing something.
LORENZO: So we are.
ANNIE: Not this! I don't want to do this.
TANYA: What do you want?
ANNIE: Not this.
LORENZO: What then?
ANNIE: I want …
TANYA: What?
ANNIE: I want …
LORENZO: Fucking hell, what!?
ANNIE: I want something!
TANYA: We all want something, Annie.
LORENZO: That's right.
ANNIE: So?
LORENZO: It's like it's some kind of revelation to you.

TANYA: We all want, Annie.
LORENZO: And some of us get what we want and some of us don't.
TANYA: Some of us deserve a lot and still get nothing.
ANNIE: So?
TANYA: It feels like you're asking for a bit much.
LORENZO: And when we put ourselves out you're ungrateful.
ANNIE: I'm not ungrateful, I'm cold.
TANYA: You're hard to please, Annie.
LORENZO: You're getting a bit demanding.
ANNIE: I'm not.
TANYA: Nothing seems to make you happy.
LORENZO: Something's always dragging you down.
TANYA: You're always down in the dumps.
LORENZO: It's like you've got no life.
TANYA: And we're watching it with our own eyes.
LORENZO: And we can't help.
TANYA: You've got to find your way out, Annie.
LORENZO: Find some strength in yourself.
TANYA: Make your own happiness.
LORENZO: Find your own peace of mind.
TANYA: We're worried about you.
LORENZO: We're being cruel to be kind.

Silence.

TANYA: It's because we love you, you know that.

SCENE NINETEEN

ANNIE *is in bed curled up in a tiny ball.*

LORENZO: The moment I saw you I thought, you are beautiful, really beautiful, so beautiful, and small. Beautiful and small. I loved you. I saw you and I couldn't keep my hands off you. Wanted to touch you, pick you up, feel your beautiful little body in my hands. Something about how little you were, how I could hold you, how I could lift you right off the ground, made me feel a big man. And a good man, a really good man. I wanted to look after you. Never wanted that before.

He looks at ANNIE.

Now look at you. Fuck. Look at you, you're nineteen and you look like an old crow. Fuck. Look at you. You used to have some pride in the way you looked, dressed up you looked beautiful. It felt good to be seen with you. Like, feast your eyes on this, and she's mine. Now who wants you, looking the way you look, who'd come near you? You're a slag, an old rag. Get up. Fucking get up, would you, you fucking useless scrag. Get up!

ANNIE: I'm sick.

LORENZO: I'm sick of you, you fucking lazy bitch. I said get up.

ANNIE: I'm sick, I'm sick, fuck you.

LORENZO: What did you say to me?

He pulls her out of the bed by her hair.

ANNIE: Tanya! Tanya!

LORENZO: Don't think Tanya doesn't feel like me. She can see how fucked you look. Have a look at yourself.

ANNIE: Tanya!

LORENZO: Don't bother calling Tanya. She doesn't care about you.

ANNIE: Tanya cares about me.

LORENZO: No she doesn't, no-one cares about you, no-one in the whole fucking world cares about you.

ANNIE: Yes they do.

LORENZO: Who?

Pause.

Who?

ANNIE: You.

LORENZO: You kidding? I don't care about you.

ANNIE: You do.

LORENZO: No.

ANNIE: You love me.

LORENZO: No, I don't love you.

ANNIE: I don't believe you.

LORENZO: It's fucking true.

ANNIE: If you don't love me you don't love anybody.

LORENZO: Yeah I do. I love plenty of people, plenty of them. I've got lots of people I love. Heaps of them. I don't need you to love.

ANNIE: Yeah you do.

LORENZO: I don't love you, no-one in their right mind could love you, not me, not Tanya, not a fucking dog could love you.
ANNIE: You do. You do. You do. You do.
LORENZO: Get dressed.
ANNIE: I'm sick.
LORENZO: You're going to work.
ANNIE: I'm sick.
LORENZO: Do something with yourself, would you? You look like shit.

SCENE TWENTY

ANNIE *stands alone.*

ANNIE: It's like this. It's not me you know and it's not anybody else either. It's me, but I'm a horse. Not just any horse. I'm beautiful. I'm fucking beautiful, I'm big, I'm black, I'm wild. But I'm not a female horse—I'm a stallion.

SCENE TWENTY-ONE

LORENZO *enters in a fury.*

LORENZO: I'm there. I'm waiting and waiting for you to come out. It gets so long I think, fuck, she's in trouble, so I go in there. And you're not there. I go in there to make sure you're alright and you've disappeared. Just like that. Gone. Leaving me, looking like a fucking idiot, like a knight who's forgotten to put on his armour and his princess has fucked off on him anyway. And you're here. What are you doing here?
ANNIE: I went out the back and came home.
LORENZO: Like I said, what are you doing here?
ANNIE: Nothing.
LORENZO: You don't get it, do you?
ANNIE: No.
LORENZO: You don't piss off on me. Right? You got that?
ANNIE: Yes, alright.
LORENZO: When I tell you you're on the job, you're on the job. You got that?
ANNIE: Yes.

LORENZO: You don't make no decisions, you don't have no opinions, you don't do anything unless I tell you to. You got that?
ANNIE: [*slightly contemptuous*] Yeah, yeah.
LORENZO: [*hurting her*] I said, you got that?
ANNIE: I got it. I got it.

>TANYA *enters, and* LORENZO *quickly moves away from* ANNIE.

TANYA: What's going on?
LORENZO: I'm trying to help her get ready for work.
ANNIE: I'm sick, I'm sick.
TANYA: You're alright, you're just run-down, that's all.
LORENZO: There's nothing wrong with her.
ANNIE: I can't.
TANYA: You're alright. You'll feel better once you're out and about.
LORENZO: That's what I've been telling her.

>ANNIE *attempts to crawl into bed.*

No you don't.

>*He pulls her out and when she struggles, he punches her. It's as if he knows as he slowly turns to face* TANYA. TANYA *has him down and is about to smash his head onto the floor.*

It was an accident! It was an accident!
ANNIE: Let him go. Tanya, let him go. Don't hurt him! Tanya, please don't hurt him.
TANYA: Go on, piss off.

>LORENZO *scurries to his feet and exits.*

Can't we fuck him off?

>ANNIE *is silent.*

He's wearing you out. He's sucking the life out of you. He's meant to look after you.
ANNIE: No he's not. That's your job. He's there to make me laugh.

>*They realise the ridiculousness of this statement and laugh.*

TANYA: Annie?
ANNIE: Mmm?
TANYA: What if …? What do you think if I …? Maybe I could do some …

ANNIE *slowly turns her head and looks at* TANYA.

I could do some …
ANNIE: I love you, Tanya. I love you.
TANYA: You know I would.
ANNIE: Yeah, of course.
TANYA: I would if I could, you know that?
ANNIE: I know that.
TANYA: As long as you know that.
ANNIE: There's no way you can do that.
TANYA: You sure?
ANNIE: It'd just about kill you, Tanya, I'm sure about that.
TANYA: As long as you know the offer's there.
ANNIE: You stick to your job I reckon.
TANYA: Alright.

Pause.

And you stick to yours, yeah?

Pause.

Yeah?
ANNIE: Yeah.

SCENE TWENTY-TWO

ANNIE *has attached herself to* LORENZO*'s leg.* TANYA *watches on.*

LORENZO: Let go. Annie, I said let go.

ANNIE *cries.*

Fucking hell, Annie, will you let me go? Tanya, do something, would you?

TANYA *shrugs.*

You brought it on yourself, Annie. You got to agree with me there, Tanya. She brought it on herself.

TANYA *shrugs.*

For Christ's sake, Annie, this was bound to happen. We're not getting on. It isn't working out. We've come to the end. We're over and there's no going back. Let go of me.

ANNIE *whimpers.*

Jesus, Annie. Come on. It just didn't last, that's all, what we had, it was good, but it didn't pull through. No big deal about that. It was good and then it was bad, no big deal. You got Tanya. Hasn't she, Tanya? She's still got you?

TANYA *is silent.*

Got to say goodbye now, baby. Got to say goodbye.

ANNIE: I'm not letting you go.

LORENZO: Don't make this ugly, Annie. Come on. Let me go.

ANNIE: I'm not letting you go.

LORENZO: Tanya, come on, help us out. Tanya, come on. It's going to get ugly, I'm telling you. What am I meant to do?

TANYA *shrugs.*

ANNIE: Give me another chance. Please, Lenny, I can make it good again. I'll be better. I've been sick. I'll work again. I'll make you happy again. Okay, Lenny, okay?

LORENZO: It's no good, Annie.

ANNIE: I love you too much. I'll be good. You'll love me again like you used to. Lenny, please. Please, Lenny. Lenny. Don't leave me.

LORENZO: [*to* TANYA] Can't you do something?

TANYA *shrugs.*

I didn't want to have to say this but you've pushed me into it. I don't love you, Annie. I thought I did but I never really did. I've found someone else and I think I do with her. I think she's the one. Yeah I do, I reckon she could be the one I love.

ANNIE and TANYA: [*together*] Who?

LORENZO: Never mind who. That's all I'm about to say. I'm sorry to have to tell you but you didn't give me any choice. I'm in love with someone else.

ANNIE and TANYA: [*together*] Who?

LORENZO: I reckon that's between her and me.

TANYA: Why? What's the big secret?

ANNIE: Who is she?

LORENZO: You don't know her.

TANYA: What's her name?

LORENZO: Greta.

TANYA: Greta?
ANNIE: Greta at the pub?
LORENZO: That's the one.

> ANNIE *lets go of* LORENZO*'s leg.*

ANNIE: [*to* TANYA] You know her, the one who works the back bar.

> TANYA *tries to place her and finally she realises who it is.*

TANYA: Oh, Greta. It's Greta you're going to. It's Greta you love.

> ANNIE *is sitting on the floor, teary and exhausted.*

LORENZO: She's the one.
ANNIE: You're such a bastard, Lenny.
TANYA: Greta's quite a catch.
LORENZO: She's alright.
ANNIE: You're such a bastard, Lenny.
LORENZO: Better go.
TANYA: Yeah.
ANNIE: No!

> LORENZO *exits.*

He was going to marry me.

SCENE TWENTY-THREE

ANNIE *and* TANYA *are alone. Silence.* ANNIE *sobs terribly.*

ANNIE: I hurt. I hurt.
TANYA: You're sick.
ANNIE: I hurt.
TANYA: You're sick.
ANNIE: [*snapping*] I'm not fucking sick!
TANYA: Alright. Alright.
ANNIE: [*in pain*] Oh, my god! Lenny.
TANYA: What do you want me to do?
ANNIE: Nothing.
TANYA: Got to be something.
ANNIE: There's nothing. What am I going to do?
TANYA: You'll get through it.
ANNIE: I won't.

TANYA: Sure you will.
ANNIE: I won't. Oh god! Lenny, why did you leave me?
TANYA: You'll be alright, Annie.
ANNIE: I won't be fucking alright!
TANYA: Alright. Alright.
ANNIE: I won't be.
TANYA: It's just a matter of time.
ANNIE: I'm not going to get over this.
TANYA: In a while, you'll see.
ANNIE: I won't see.
TANYA: It feels like this now, Annie, but you'll see in a while you'll …
ANNIE: No I won't! I fucking won't!
TANYA: Alright! Alright!
ANNIE: You don't know how I feel!
TANYA: Fucking hell, that's it.
ANNIE: It's just that I'm hurting a bit.
TANYA: I've had it.
ANNIE: I'll get over it.
TANYA: You're fucking shitting me.
ANNIE: Tanya, I'm sorry. I'm sick.
TANYA: You're shitting me.
ANNIE: I'm sick. I'm so sick. Help me. Tanya? Help me.

ANNIE collapses into TANYA's arms.

SCENE TWENTY-FOUR

Silence. TANYA *watches* ANNIE.

TANYA: You look good. Better. Not so yellow. We'll go soon. When you stop sleeping all the time. When you buck up. Get out of this hole. Talked to snotty nose? I been. She's a bitch. She been getting to you?
ANNIE: No.
TANYA: Sure?
ANNIE: She shits me.
TANYA: Yeah.
ANNIE: All the questions shit me.
TANYA: Don't tell her too much.
ANNIE: I don't.

TANYA: Don't tell her anything.
ANNIE: I don't.
TANYA: Tell her stuff she wants to hear.
ANNIE: Like what?
TANYA: They love to hear how you've been fucked. I tell her that. Big breakthrough, she thinks.
ANNIE: You don't.
TANYA: I tell her my father fucked me, my uncle fucked me, my brothers fucked me, my mum's boyfriends fucked me I tell her, and the more fucks I tell her about the more her mouth falls open.
ANNIE: If I told her who fucked me I'd be there till Christmas. I can't remember how many I've fucked. I've been fucking since I was nine years old. For ten years I've been fucking. Fucking hell, that's a lot of fucking when you think about it.
TANYA: Yeah, well, so what?
ANNIE: Nothing, except it's a lot, that's all.
TANYA: Yeah, well, so it's a lot.
ANNIE: Well, you were talking about you being fucked and all I'm saying is I've been fucked a lot.
TANYA: Yeah?
ANNIE: Well, you stopped.
TANYA: Yeah, so you've been fucked more. It's not a fucking competition, Annie.
ANNIE: I know it's not.
TANYA: I stopped because I made them stop.
ANNIE: Yeah, alright, alright.
TANYA: What do you talk about?
ANNIE: Nothing much. Mum sometimes.
TANYA: Oh, she'd like that. You don't cry, do you?
ANNIE: No.
TANYA: That's what they want you to do. It shits them when you don't.
ANNIE: I never cry. She says that to me sometimes, she says, you're allowed to cry, Annie. I think, what the fuck.
TANYA: About what?
ANNIE: What?
TANYA: What does she want you to cry about?
ANNIE: Nothing.

TANYA: What's wrong?
ANNIE: Nothing.
TANYA: What's fucking wrong?
ANNIE: Nothing I said.
TANYA: Don't shit me. It shits me when you say nothing when there's something.
ANNIE: It's bullshit.
TANYA: It's me you're talking to, Annie. It's me.
ANNIE: It's really bullshit.
TANYA: What!?
ANNIE: She says you're taking advantage of me.

Pause.

TANYA: I'm taking advantage of you?
ANNIE: Because I do all the sex.
TANYA: Of course you do. Of course you bloody do. That bitch is trying to fuck us up.
ANNIE: I'm just a bit tired.
TANYA: She's got at you because you're weak. They go for who's weak. Who looks after you?
ANNIE: You do.
TANYA: Who fucking makes all the arrangements?
ANNIE: You.
TANYA: Who's there when there's trouble?
ANNIE: You.
TANYA: Do I make you do stuff you don't want to do?
ANNIE: No.
TANYA: Do I make sure there's never any heavy shit?
ANNIE: Yeah.
TANYA: Do I knock you around?
ANNIE: No.
TANYA: Do we split everything down the middle?
ANNIE: Yeah.
TANYA: Have I ever left you and gone off to score.
ANNIE: No.
TANYA: Fucking hell, Annie, who stuck by you when you got sick when you looked like shit when you were so out of it you wouldn't know nothing about nothing?

ANNIE: I'm still a bit sick, that's all.

TANYA: I'm taking advantage of you. That bitch is jealous that's what. She doesn't understand a thing about us. She thinks you're a slut, she thinks I'm … fuck knows what she thinks I am. She feels sorry for us, poor things, that's what we are, poor, poor things. She doesn't get it that we can love each other, that we can actually love each other. Poor, poor fucking things don't love. We're takers, users, bastards, arseholes.

ANNIE: Leave it go now. It's crap. It just got stuck in my head. It just got stuck there. She stuck it there and I'm sorry.

TANYA: Yeah yeah. Yeah yeah.

ANNIE: Let me kiss you.

TANYA: Hang on a bit.

ANNIE: Why can't I kiss you?

TANYA: I need a breather.

ANNIE: Come on, Tanya, this is crap. I'm your love.

TANYA: I don't feel good. I didn't have to think before. Just was. Don't feel good.

ANNIE: You will.

TANYA: It's like getting a smudge off glass.

ANNIE: Don't do this.

TANYA: You said it.

ANNIE: Yeah, I said it.

TANYA: You felt it.

Pause.

ANNIE: Yeah, I felt it.

TANYA: Jesus, Annie.

ANNIE: I did.

TANYA: That's not going to go away. Is it?

SCENE TWENTY-FIVE

ANNIE *stands alone.*

ANNIE: I'm standing on this ridge and I'm looking out way before me— hundreds of kilometres of sandy desert stretches below. I'm standing looking out across it as though it's mine. I've done battle in it and won. I've courted in it, I've danced across it and I've run it—with unbelievable speed—neck stretched to breaking, sweat pouring and hearing the pounding of my hooves beneath me.

TANYA *steps forward.*

TANYA: Where am I?
ANNIE: I'm alone. It's just me.
TANYA: No, I'm there with you.
ANNIE: No you're not. I told you, it's just me.
TANYA: No, you may not see me, but I tell you I'm there.
ANNIE: You're not fucking there, Tanya!
TANYA: Oh, yes I am. You'd like that, wouldn't you—your fucking neck stretched out and your pounding—just you, not me, oh no, just you, alone. I am there. You know where I am? Can't you guess? Why do you think you're doing all that pounding? Because I'm there, my heels half buried in your flanks and I'm riding you. Don't you feel me pulling at the bit in your mouth?
ANNIE: Shut up, Tanya! You're not there and what I'm doing has nothing to do with you.
TANYA: Why not? Why aren't I there? Where am I then? Tell me that! What have you done with me?

SCENE TWENTY-SIX

TANYA *falls back on the bed.*

ANNIE: Where's mine?
TANYA: You've been sick.
ANNIE: Yeah, so?
TANYA: It's a waste then, isn't it?
ANNIE: I'll be the judge of that.
TANYA: There's plenty more out there.
ANNIE: How did you pay for it?
TANYA: Credit.
ANNIE: Oh yeah. So I'm supposed to pay for that, am I? What if I've had enough of that? What then?
TANYA: Who's forcing you?
ANNIE: You are.
TANYA: No, you do what you want.

ANNIE: I might just do that.
TANYA: Who's stopping you?
ANNIE: You are.
TANYA: That's where you're wrong, Annie, if you don't want to do something, don't.
ANNIE: Who's going to pay off the credit?
TANYA: I will.
ANNIE: Yeah, how?
TANYA: I'll pay.
ANNIE: No, it'll be me who pays.
TANYA: I said I'll pay.
ANNIE: I always pay.
TANYA: Then don't. From now on, don't. Got it? It's clear.
ANNIE: Yeah, clear as fucking mud. I know how it goes. I know that it'll be me who ends up paying, it always is, me, paying, for you.
TANYA: Fuck you, you don't keep me.
ANNIE: Actually I do.
TANYA: You keep me? I don't think so. I do everything for you. One moment I'm your fucking nurse, next I'm your servant, I'm your bloody bloke, I'm your best friend, I'm your only fucking friend. And I don't care because that's what you do when you love someone. You know that? That's what you do.

SCENE TWENTY-SEVEN

ANNIE: Has it gone?

   Pause.

TANYA: It's still there.
ANNIE: Really?
TANYA: Yeah.
ANNIE: Is it?
TANYA: Sure.
ANNIE: Where?
TANYA: It's somewhere.
ANNIE: Where, Tanya, where is it?
TANYA: I don't know.
ANNIE: Fucking hell.

TANYA: It'll turn up.
ANNIE: Will it?
TANYA: I don't know.
ANNIE: You still love me? A little bit? Do you? Just a little bit? Heh? Come on, a little bit, I reckon you do. I reckon you love me a little bit. A tiny little bit. Heh? Am I right? The tiniest bit. Heh? What do you reckon? Love me a bit? Just a bit. Love me? Tanya? Love me? Love me. Love me. Love me.

SCENE TWENTY-EIGHT

ANNIE *and* TANYA *stand holding hands.*

ANNIE: We're carp.
TANYA: What?
ANNIE: Carp.
TANYA: What the fuck's carp?
ANNIE: Goldfish, but gone huge. And not beautiful, not gold anymore. Huge fucking ugly fish. Monster fish.
TANYA: I'm not fucking carp.
ANNIE: Yeah, you are. We're carp.
TANYA: I'm not fucking carp.
ANNIE: I saw them in the creek, the water was low and I saw them. Huge fuckers, a school of them making a racket. Slapping the top of the water, caught in this shitty water, huge and desperate, time running out on them.
TANYA: I'm not fucking carp.
ANNIE: You are. And me too.

    Silence.

THE END

SLUT

SLUT was first produced by Platform Youth Theatre as part of a double program of plays called *Tenderness* on 7 March 2008 at fortyfivedownstairs, Melbourne, with the following cast:

LOLITA	Chloe Boreham
CHORUS	Maysa Abouzeid
	Camille Lopez
	Anastasia Baboussouras
	Luke Frazer

Director, Nadja Kostich
Designer, Marg Horwell
Lighting Designer, Richard Vabre
Sound Designer, Kelly Ryall
Choreographer, Tony Yap

CHARACTERS

LOLITA

CHORUS OF YOUNG WOMEN

A CHORUS *of young women sit in judgement.*

CHORUS: A man is dead.
    An innocent man.
    A man with a wife and kids.
    Three of them.
    Two boys and a girl.
    A good man.
    Not someone not worth anything.
    Not some deadbeat.
    Not some homeless bloke.
    Some drunk.
    Some useless junkie.
    Not someone old.
    A good man.
    A really good man.
    A man worth a lot.
    A man with a job.
    A good job.
    With responsibilities.
    Someone important.
    Dead.
    Just like that.
    Suddenly.
    Dead.
    An innocent bystander.
    A total stranger.
    His only crime is he wants to help.
    To save Lolita.
    To do the right thing.
    He didn't even know her.
    To offer a hand.
    To save Lolita.
    A good citizen.
    Didn't hesitate.
    He put his life at risk.

To save Lolita.
A brave man.
Admirable.
Selfless.
A hero.
Dead.
A dead man.
Definitely a dead man.

LOLITA *is riding a bike. She rides hard and her hair streams back in the wind.*

LOLITA: I like it. I like it a lot.
 I like it this fast.
 I like it that if I fell I'd die.
 I like the sound of my breath.
 Like the ache in my legs.
 Like the way the wind matts up my hair.
 Like the sweat on my face and the cold air.
 Like the whirring wheels, the clicking gears, the hum in my ears.
 I like the smell of me.
 I like the feel of my heartbeat.
 I like it that I can't think.
 If I think, I'll fall.
 I'll pedal into a hole.
 If I think I'll find myself in a ditch, I'll smack into the back of a truck, wrap myself around a pole.
 It's lovely not thinking, not caring, having one problem; staying on my bike.
 Lovely life. Lovely, lovely life. That's what you say on a bike. That's what I said, I reckon. Until the day I stopped, and didn't ride my bike anymore.
 I was nine.

 LOLITA *stops.*

CHORUS: We've known Lolita for a long time.
 We've known her since we were kids.

We went to the same crèche.
I lived next door.
We went to the same primary school.
She was my best friend.
We know her through and through.
We know everything there is to know about her.
We know Lolita better than anyone.
We were that close.
When we were babies Lolita and I had our photos taken together at Kmart.
When we were one, we were put in the same cot because I had measles so Lolita could catch them too.
When we were two, Lolita and I went missing. We were found two hours later in a crèche cupboard, sleeping.
When we were three, we painted each other blue.
When we were four, Lolita and I held hands and tiptoed towards the deep end of the Northcote pool and as the water was about to cover our noses, a lifeguard dived in and saved us.
When we were five, Lolita and I drank a bottle of medicine and had our stomachs pumped.
When we were six, Lolita and I danced in fairy dresses at the Sunday school pageant.
When we were seven, Lolita and I buried her brother's pet guinea-pig alive. His name was Kevin.
When we were eight, we smoked one of my dad's cigarettes and got sick.
Everything changed.
When Lolita was nine.

The CHORUS *shift into a conspiratorial bunch.*

It happened really fast.
It was very sudden.
There was nothing to be done.
There was no turning back.
These things just happen.
They can't be helped.
It wasn't Lolita's fault.

It was after the holidays.
The Christmas ones.
And the start of Grade Four.
We came back to school.
As usual.
And Lolita…
Had tits.
Breasts.
Real breasts.
Huge ones.
At first, I thought it was a joke.
That she was having us on.
That she had a padded bra on.
Because nothing else had changed.
She was a little girl with tits.
Her breasts were frightening.
They were.
My mother said it was unnatural.
A little girl with tits.
It was kind of ridiculous.
Boys went into a frenzy.
They almost licked their lips.
'Look, look, Lolita's got tits.'
They were mesmerised by them.
I was mesmerised by them.
They couldn't take their eyes off them.
I couldn't take my eyes off them.
They were beautiful.
They were.
They'd comment on them.
They'd almost talk to them.
Sometimes they'd grab at them.
And Lolita let them.

Pause.

And something else had changed.
Lolita had been smart.

Really smart.
Like at maths smart.
She always got the top mark.
And she could spell.
She was top of the class.
She read chapter books before any of us.
She got dumb.
Not all at once.
Gradually.
In the same year.
So dumb it was easy to forget she'd been smart.
Dumb.
Even I got better marks.
Failing maths, which she'd never done.
You wondered if she'd never been smart.
Or her smartness had run out.
Couldn't do her sums.
Couldn't read out loud.
Didn't know the answers.
Didn't seem to care.
She could've been faking it.
For a while I think she was.
Then she really was.
She was.
Dumb.
   Pause.
In Grade Five, we had Mr Markham.
He was young. For a teacher.
He loved Lolita.
He did.
She was teacher's pet.
He stared at her all the time.
He smiled at her.
He held her hand every chance he could get.
He teased her.
He whispered in her ear.
He squeezed her.

He gave her sweets.
Sometimes he'd show off in front of her.
He would laugh and tell jokes to her.
He would lean over her and help her with her sums and sweat would suddenly appear on his top lip.
Once he lifted Barry Dansen by the arm and held him dangling.
Barry had teased Lolita.
He called Barry a dirty little rat and dropped him outside in the corridor—like that.
Mr Markham loved Lolita.
We'd witnessed how the boys had reacted.
But this was something different.
This was a grown man.
A teacher.
We watched as he became besotted with Lolita.
We'd all by then experienced being looked at.
For too long.
Too intensely.
By men who passed by in the street.
By a girlfriend's father.
By a grandfather.
We'd all by then experienced the touch.
From some old mate of your father who hugged too close.
From someone at church who held your hand and rubbed your palm with his thumb.
From an uncle who put his arm around you and placed his fingertips on the edge of your breast.
From a shopkeeper who holds onto your fingers when he gives you your change.
We'd all by then experienced a kiss from an adult that was way too wet.
A tongue that suddenly slips between your lips.
We'd all by then experienced the confusion of how it feels.
The attention.
How strange it is.
Is this being liked?
Is this meant to be nice?

But this was something different.
Lolita and Mr Markham were teaching us a far more sophisticated lesson.
We learned a lot.
We learned something we'd never known.
Though it was quite mystifying at the time.
It was.
It was no easy lesson.
It was hard to know quite what was going on.
Lolita seemed to be the only one who knew.
And Mr Markham.
He definitely knew.
They were a great study.
They were.
Fascinating.
Lolita, in particular, we observed.
She never flinched when Mr Markham touched her.
Whatever look he gave her, she returned.
Lolita smiled back.
She'd laugh loudly, exuberantly.
Lolita talked back.
She'd whisper too.
She'd pout sometimes.
Lolita enjoyed Mr Markham and his attentions.
I was jealous of her, often.
I was too.
It was truly amazing to watch her.
Lolita, somehow, knew exactly what to do.

LOLITA *is in a rowing boat. She pulls at the oars.*

LOLITA: Not once did I row the boat. At first, I thought it must have been because I was young, until one day my younger brother was given the oars. I thought it must have been because I was too weak but my younger brother was smaller than me. I thought it was because I never asked but nor did my younger brother ask. In fact, I could tell he didn't really want to. He was happy to spend the time drawing a line in the water with his hand. I didn't really want to row either, not until my younger brother was handed the oars did I want to. I saw myself. I knew I'd be good at it. I knew I would make perfect, balanced, easy strokes, which would have the boat slide across the surface of the water. This was something I could do, see myself, at various tasks, and know that I would be good at them. I could see myself chop wood for instance; I knew I could get into the rhythm of splitting the wood with one swing. I could see myself abseiling down a cliff. I knew I would find my footing, be able to co-ordinate the ropes and use the momentum to bound down the face of it. I could see myself doing lots of things. Climbing, running, skidding, swimming, jumping over things. Rarely was I given the opportunity to use my strength, to test my power, to exert myself. Rarely have I ever run out of breath. Rarely was I called outside to push our clapped-out car, or to climb the tree to get the cat, or to mow, or dig, or to even put the bin out. I don't know whether I wanted to be asked to do these things. I don't think I did. One Sunday I got up and my dad and my brothers had gone fishing without me. I don't remember Dad telling me I was no longer invited, nor do I remember telling him I no longer wanted to go. It didn't particularly upset me. Perhaps he thought I didn't want to. Perhaps I didn't. Perhaps I thought I was too old. I was twelve.

    LOLITA *rows out of sight.*

CHORUS: Lolita took high school by storm.
    And we got swept along.
    She led us down the corridors.
    We were like miniature warriors.
    She was full of sudden high-pitched screams.
    Shrieks and ear-splitting squeals.
    One moment she'd laugh almost hysterically.
    Then she'd laugh in loud, mad guffaws.
    She'd giggle and not be able to stop.
    She'd be put outside the principal's door.
    She'd laugh and laugh and laugh some more.
    And we'd join her.
    It was over the top.

It was delirious.
It was contagious.
It was crazy.
It was totally meaningless.
It was fun.
It was.
She was hilarious.
Lolita drew laughter from almost anyone.
And she drew attention.
Lolita was known by the entire school.
Everyone was drawn to her.
Boys in particular.
They loved her.
They did.
Boys of all sizes.
Some not grown yet.
Some with beards.
They'd wait for her outside the classroom door.
They'd pass her notes.
They'd beg her to meet them after school.
They'd declare their love for her on every blackboard.
One wrote, 'I love Lolita' on one of the school's walls.
She received fat love letters in the mail.
One of them was willing to die for her, he was that serious.
Lolita met them on the oval.
At the bus stop.
At the 7-Eleven.
At lunchtimes.
After school.
They walked her home.
They would constantly ring her.
And text her.
They would wait outside her house in the chance they might see her.
There was barely a moment when she wasn't pursued.
They loved her.
They did.
Sometimes I was jealous.

So was I.
Because we also loved Lolita.

   Pause.

Lolita introduced us to feminine ways.
She was the first to pluck her eyebrows.
She plucked them thin, in an arch that gave her face a constant look of surprise.
She was the first to shave her legs.
She never wore socks or stockings so her legs were completely shining bare.
She'd been wearing make-up for years.
Her face was almost orange at times. And it would stop sharply along her jawline.
She was constantly repainting her lips.
Her lashes were thick.
She was the first to pierce her tongue.
I wasn't even allowed to have my ears done.
She dyed her hair all colours.
She liked regrowth. She thought it made her look older.
Lolita was the first to smoke cigarettes.
She liked the look of a cigarette in her hand, she said.
She was the first to smoke a joint.
She liked how it made her light in the head.
She was the first to get drunk.
She sat in the gutter and vomited all over her brand-new dress.
She was the first to shave her pubic hair.
She hated hair down there.
So do I.
She said men preferred it if we looked like little girls.
She was first to give head.
She just closed her eyes, she said.
Lolita was the first to have sex.
She chose carefully.
She could have her pick.
She chose a boy in Year Twelve.
We liked his name.
Andreas.

We all agreed on him.
He was nearly a man.
He had a reputation.
For breaking hearts.
And hymens.
We agreed that he was definitely the one.
He'd know what he was doing, she thought.
He'd had practice.
And he was handsome.
He was.
We were very excited.
She arranged everything.
It was like she was making a doctor's appointment.
The date, the time, the place.
It was all confirmed.
We waited.
We were beside ourselves.
It was so exhilarating, the waiting, it was painful.
We waited.
To hear every detail.
To be taken through it step by step.
To relish every shocking moment.
We knew it would be delicious.
Lolita finally came.
And we squealed and danced around her.
Like we were in some weird ritual.
We screamed and laughed liked maniacs when she tried to speak.
We wanted to know.
And we didn't.
We wanted to draw it out.
To take pleasure in the anticipation.
We wanted her to tell.
And didn't.
Perhaps we sensed the disappointment.
When finally we were silent.
Lolita had little to say.
It was okay.

Is what she said.
It was nothing much.
We were kind of sad.
It was suddenly awkward.
Suddenly silent.
Lolita suddenly looked her age.
She was twelve.

    Pause.

Our disappointment was short-lived.
Lolita made up for it for sure.
She was a champion.
A rebel.
A star.
Her sexual exploits were numerous.
They were famous.
Stories of them delighted us.
Her life was so full it filled ours.
We loved her life.
We envied her freedom.
We were in awe of her power.
She'd strut.
She'd stick her tits out.
She'd hold her head up.
She was unafraid.
Lolita was the most amazing slut.
She was.
And we loved her.
She was never ashamed of anything she did.
Shame was something Lolita did not believe in.
She was lucky.
She was.
Lolita had no secrets.
She shared everything.
Nothing kept in.
All of us.
And everyone else.
Knew everything.

A CHORUS MEMBER *detaches herself from the group.*

CHORUS MEMBER: Lolita and I stayed with my grandmother in the country during the Christmas holidays. I'd invited Lolita a few months earlier and now I was dreading it. My grandmother was old, her house was nowhere near a town, she didn't have a television, and there was nothing, absolutely nothing to do. On the train, I warned Lolita. I told her, you might want to go home. You might only want to stay a few days. You can go whenever you want to, you know? When you've had enough just say so. For three weeks me and Lolita swam every day in my grandma's dam. Every day we picked leeches off each other before we swam again. One day we took off our bathers and covered each other completely in mud. We baked dry and when we moved we cracked. Lolita said we were coming out of our shells. Born again, anew. Every day we looked for lizards and one day we found a snake and scrammed. We sat on warm rocks and sang bits of songs. We helped my grandma in the garden, with the cooking, with feeding the animals. At nights we played Scrabble and pieced together old jigsaws. We listened to music, we listened to the radio, we listened to my grandma's stories and finally we came home. We were fourteen.

Pause.

CHORUS: Year Nine.
The year of the bitch.

They howl.

We ran in packs.
Snarling, teeth bared, looking for a kill.

They howl.

A fat girl.
A girl who thinks her shit don't stink.
A girl with no dress sense.
A girl who's top of the class.
A girl with bad skin.
A pretty girl.
They didn't have a chance in hell.
The pack would change constantly.

Turn on one of their own.
Tear her limb from limb.
We'd split and reform and split again.
We'd devour each other one day.
And the next day, declare each other best friends.
Every day there were tears.
Someone hysterically sobbing.
Every day some girl would get clobbered.
You told her, and she told me, and now you're dead meat.
We talked behind each other's backs.
Every day we'd confess.
To some crime against the other.
We'd declare love for each other.
We'd tell each other we were shit.

They turn on each other.

You were such a bitch.
I hated you.
You were a liar.
You couldn't be trusted.
You'd tell everyone's secrets.
You told her that I thought she was shit.
And you told her, she was a fuckwit.
You said I was ugly.
You said I was dumb.
It was fun.
It was.

Pause.

And we turned against Lolita.
She thought she was better than us.
She thought she was so hot.
She honestly thought she was what the boys wanted.
She thought she could have them all.
She was too much.
Lolita didn't care who she fucked.
Her boyfriend.
Or hers.

Or hers.
Or mine.
Once, I told her, keep your hands off him, would you, he's taken.
All that did was excite her.
That night she took him home with her.
Lolita was insatiable.
She was.
Her appetite was unbelievable.
She was a slut.
But I'll tell you something about Lolita.
What?
She's never had an orgasm.
Of course she has.
No, she hasn't.
She loves fucking.
She does.

They're in for the kill.

Lolita's laughter grew irritating.
Her wild giggling was fake.
Her shrieking and screeching, infuriating.
I saw her on a crowded bus, talking at the top of her voice, saying fuck this, fuck that.
I saw her giving head to some bloke in the park.
I saw her mauling this guy on the train station.
I saw her with two boys, their hands all over her.
I saw her having sex in the back of a car.
I saw her at a party lift up her top and her tits were falling out of her bra.
I saw her get into a car with four men who were strangers.
She was outrageous.
She was out of control.
She was shameless.
She had no self-respect.
She was no good.
She had no morals.
None.
She had a couple of bouts of STDs.

She did.
She was disgusting.
Over the top.
She was frightening.
She was.
She'd done it with almost everyone.
Such a slut.

Pause.

It was time for us to give Lolita up.
It was.
It took some time to shake her.
Nobody actually told her.
We let her know gradually.
We stopped waiting for her.
We never spoke unless we had to.
We avoided eye contact with her.
We stopped talking when she approached.
We never laughed at her jokes.
We winced at her squealing.
We were never outwardly mean.
But we were as cruel as we could be.
But it wasn't until the party.
Then it was clear.
Her time was up.
Well and truly.
We let Lolita go completely.

Pause.

The party is a Year Eleven one.
It's crowded and people are packed in and spill out into the backyard where some unsuspecting parent has hung a marquee from the clothes line.
There's a tacky banner with 'Happy Sixteenth Birthday Damian' written in dripping black paint.
The party is pumping.
Lolita is already drunk and dancing and as usual drawing a lot of attention.

Her skirt has ridden up.
She's taken off her top and tossed it at someone.
And her breasts are shaking themselves out of her bra.
Gatecrashers come from the local pub and the party is bulging at the sides.
Having older men there makes it extra exciting.
They're standing around watching Lolita.
And she's giving them the performance of her life.
A group of boys are pissed and an argument breaks out.
One of them has drunk another's beer.
The argument turns into a fight.
Someone throws a punch.
A can is thrown at someone's head.
The party scatters in a panic of broken glass and spilled plates of cabana and cheese.
Someone's got a nosebleed.
Someone has a cut over his eye.
Someone else is screaming.
Someone is vomiting under the lemon tree.
Lolita has disappeared.
The fight has calmed but there remains a feeling of unfinished business.
Any moment it'll start again.
We try to calm some of the boys down.
We try to patch up some of their wounds.
We try to divert their attention.
To get the party moving again.
But their chests are puffed up in outrage.
Their tempers are flaring.
This isn't the time for girls.
It's danger time.
Time to get out of there.
Time to disappear.
We look out for each other.
We give each other the sign.
We collect our bags.
We hid them under some bushes when we arrived.

We follow each other through the shattered glass past Damian's torn-down birthday sign.
We go inside.
We go quickly through the kitchen.
Where a bloke is spewing in the sink.
We make our way through the lounge room which is strangely empty.
We thread our way along the hall.
And realise then that something's odd.
A whole lot of men are lined up along the wall.
In a queue.
Waiting to go through one of the bedroom doors.
And immediately we know what's going on.
Lolita.
She's inside.
And the men are lined up for her.
We don't stop.
We keep on until we're out the front door, through the front garden, out the gate and onto the street.
We keep walking.
No-one is talking.
The sound of Lolita's screams still rings in our ears.

A long silence.

LOLITA *stands draped with a white cloth. She is dressed in white. She stands in an ethereal light.*

LOLITA: I don't remember a single dream. Not one. I never had one. I never thought, one day I will be something, I will be a famous something or other. I will be a model or an actress on TV. I will be a princess or a singer or a ballet dancer. I never imagined myself in any situation. I never saw myself in another place or another country or anywhere really. I didn't imagine anything about myself. I don't think I did much imagining at all. I didn't imagine any kind of fantasy land or out-of-space place. I didn't imagine. I just didn't. I didn't know how to. I didn't know that I should or could or that's what most people do. I don't remember ever wanting something. Badly wanting something. I've wanted things like a pair of shoes or a lipstick or a slice of pizza. I've never wanted anything more complicated. I can't think of anything to want for. I think only of silly things, things you can buy at a shop. I suppose I want to be liked. I want that. I'd like to be liked. That's it. That's all. And … And, I want to want more.

LOLITA *fades in the light.*

CHORUS: Lolita dropped out of school.
No huge surprise.
Not at all.
We didn't really see Lolita anymore.
Hardly at all.
Her friendship was really difficult to sustain.
The trouble with Lolita is that she thought she could have it all. She thought she could be the same. But you can't possibly get away with it. You give it up and you're a slut.
That's it.
That's how it is.
We're not the same as Lolita.
We're not.
No way.
Every now and then there was news of Lolita.
This still caused some excitement.
Though nothing like the old days.
Lolita had got herself a man.
The one man.
A real man.
Older.
Tougher.
A huge man.
A man with tatts.
I love tattoos.
Not like now tattoos.
Homemade tatts.
Prison tatts.
Tatts that make you shiver.
He was tough, really tough.
Sexy tough.

And he loved Lolita.
He did.
Well done, Lolita.
He seemed good for her.
A relationship.
For the first time, Lolita was with one man.
Like finally she found someone.
She'd met her match.
Finally she'd settled down.
She'd been tamed.
It seemed romantic.
They were in love.
Lolita had someone to look after her.
A mature man.
It suited her.
We felt good for her.
Then I saw him with Lolita. I was working the drive-in at Macca's and she and him drove in. He ordered. Lolita sat beside him and looked like a scared little kid.
And I saw him. I still lived next door but Lolita was rarely in. I was waving my boyfriend off when I heard her scream. He was pulling Lolita down the path by her hair.
I saw him with Lolita at a club. He jerked her hand behind her back and forced her to her knees.
I saw Lolita running from him.
It was like she was owned by him.
Lolita was never going to be someone who was ordinary.
It was always going to be wild with her.
Always going to be out of control.
She was never going to do what's normal.
Not Lolita.

> LOLITA *is lying on what now is clearly a hospital bed, dressed in a hospital gown.*

A good man.
Not someone not worth anything.
An innocent bystander.
A man with a wife and kids.

Tries to save Lolita.
And is shot dead.
Lolita and her boyfriend had been out clubbing.
And drinking, and dancing, and snorting cocaine.
She was wearing something skimpy.
There's an argument and the tough man is in a rage.
Lolita tries to run away.
But he runs after her.
There's always excitement with Lolita.
And this really good man.
Tries to save her and is shot.
And Lolita tries to run.
And she too is shot.
It's always wild with Lolita.
In the papers they call her a party girl.
I suppose they can't call her a slut.
She might die.
They say she's on her deathbed.
Better.
What?
Better she dies, I reckon.
Be hard to live.
Don't know how she could.
She couldn't.
Couldn't face it.
Couldn't live with herself.
Couldn't bear the weight of it.
She'd want to hide away.
To die in shame.
Better to hear nothing more of her.
It is.

 LOLITA *disappears.*

 Pause.

It is.

THE END

From left: Rachel Burke as Olivia, Miranda Daughtry as Annie and Anna Steen as Ruby, in the State Theatre Company South Australia's 2018 production of IN THE CLUB. (Photo: Sia Duff)

In the Club

In the Club was first produced by the State Theatre Company South Australia at the Odeon Theatre, Adelaide, on 23 February 2018 with the following cast:

OLIVIA	Rachel Burke
ANNIE	Miranda Daughtry
ANGUS	Rashidi Edward
SEAN	Dale March
JAMES	Nathan O'Keefe
RUBY	Anna Steen

Director, Geordie Brookman
Associate Director, Suzannah Kennett Lister
Set and Lighting Designers, Geoff Cobham and Chris Petridis
Costume Design, State Theatre Company Wardrobe
Music, Gazelle Twin (UK)

CHARACTERS

ANNIE
OLIVIA   three women out on the town
RUBY

ANGUS
SEAN   three men looking to let their hair down
JAMES

A CHORUS OF MEN

SETTING

A club, a dance floor, women's toilets, a bar, a laneway, a bedroom.

An image of an ultrasound. The heart of a foetus beats at an enormous rate.

ANNIE *stands in light.*

ANNIE: At five, at ten, at fifteen, I didn't have a clue. Not really. Of course, I knew. I knew but I didn't. At sixteen, I knew. Oh, I knew then. But only one year before, I didn't. Never thought about it, never entered my head, which is strange I guess because when I was fifteen was when I first bled. You'd think that would drive it home, that would put it out there, make it known. But no. At sixteen, it was clear to me. It was made clear to me. I was a girl.

I didn't think I was a boy. I wasn't hankering to be one of them, wasn't wishing I had a dick or had no tits, though I must admit I wasn't keen on my tits. They got in my way.

I had a dream. Hang on, a dream's wrong. A dream might not come true and I knew I was going to be someone, going to achieve something, going to do something great. I knew that from such a young age. Never doubted it. Not for a moment did I think I was being fanciful or delusional or just a silly kid with ideas too big. I thought I can be anyone I want to be, do anything I want to do. What could stop me?

I don't know a single woman who has kept a childhood dream alive. All their dreams are dead, way dead, died so long ago they barely remember them. Perhaps they never had them. No-one in my family, in my street, at my school—all their dreams either stayed inside their heads or morphed into some bullshit about marriage and kids.

For the first fifteen years of my life I was a bird in flight, I was a gazelle running across the steppes, I was a cheetah, a leopard, a wild dog. I was agile, swift, lithe, dangerous. I moved with grace. My reflexes were startlingly quick. It was as if I had an extra sense. I had extraordinary strength. For the first fifteen years of my life, I was totally in my body, testing it, pushing it, training it to endure, to last the distance. I ran and I leapt fences and carried enormous weights on my back. I had persistence. There wasn't a game I couldn't play. My body felt no restraint. I encouraged it, talked to it, told it to do more, to roar, to exalt in the pleasure of it, to ignore the pain, to feel it soar. Never felt afraid. Never held back. I was invincible. I was going to make the grade one day. Not once did I give my gender a thought.

At sixteen, that was taken away.

It's strange how little it took to have that self, that being, that person stolen from me. So quick. Gone. Just like that. Snap.

My football team—my boys, I'd call them. My boys. I knew everything about them, knew each player like the back of my hand as they say. I knew everything about the game. I went with my dad to every match where we screamed and hollered and cursed the umpire, where we talked about the level of play endlessly, where we wept when one of my boys leapt into the air and took an amazing mark to boot it seamlessly through the sticks. My boys. They were me. They were what I was going to be, an athlete who would bring a stadium roaring to its feet. I understood them; I grieved for them when their bodies betrayed them, a hammy, an ACL, a fucked knee. My boys were champions, were good and brave. Like me.

I'm sixteen. At school. It's the most exciting day of my life. Some of my boys are coming to school to give a talk. My heart's in my mouth. My heart's thumping about. My heart's … about to break.

Three giants walk into the school gym and take up all the space. We lift our chins to see their fine heads, their chiselled features, their eyes which sparkle because they know they're loved. More than loved. Adored. They're full of themselves. They move easily and their smiles charm us. They've got gorgeous pluck. Three young bucks, three brave warriors, gods they are and I know them, I've watched them play for years. They're my boys and I'm proud of them.

The girls, they go berserk. These are girls who hate footy, who never watch a match. These are girls who scream and turn away from the ball when it's thrown to them. These are girls when forced to play, huddle together and talk, girls who run all awkward, are inexplicably slow, are suddenly unco. Girls who don't give a shit about sport. But here they are, giggling and fawning and talking baby talk. Here they are smiling coyly, biting their bottom lips and shoving out their tits. What's going on, I think? And I'm thick because it takes me some time to realise that this is full-on flirting, that this is not about footy, this is about the boys, mine, and I'm embarrassed for them girls. I am.

The girls are asking them what car they drive, what bands they like, whether they watch some reality TV crap. Our sports teacher's useless; he's equally starstruck. I try to bring them back, to keep them on track. I ask them a question about the team. I ask them about a game they played when they got smashed, I ask them if they can give any advice to other sports-minded people like me. They barely answer me. They don't look at me. Their eyes and ears for the girls, the girls with their giggles, their pouting lips, the weird swaying of their hips. My boys have got themselves caught in a spider's web, well and truly twisted up in its sticky threads.

The bell rings and the girls hang about and there's some leaning in close and whispering stuff. They go at last and my boys walk to the car park. I follow them. I talk non-stop: I want them to know that I'm nothing like them girls, that I'm one of them—clear-headed, disciplined, focussed—I want them to know how many medals I've won how many ribbons I've had pinned on my chest how I've been sussed out by scouts I want them to know how good I am I'm talking non-stop because they're getting in their car and they're going and they don't know anything about me and I'm desperate for them to. I ask one of my boys for his number then, before they go and I never see them again. Maybe we can catch up I say to Sean O'Grady, a mid-fielder we recruited last season. I feel this rush of blood to my head and know I've turned bright red. And I can't believe it, he takes my phone and keys it in.

I turn up at the flat. Someone I don't recognise answers the door and I wander in. Music so loud I think it'll bust my head. A young man with a skimpy towel barely covering his bits runs from one room to another. On the balcony, a group of men are taking sausages from a sizzling barbecue and sticking them in bread. One guy plays PlayStation on the settee. I think, what am I doing here? And I don't know except I've come for something. There's something I want. I find Sean. He's in bed. I'm standing in the doorway looking pretty stupid, I'm sure. He pulls back the covers and says: Get in.

Is this it?

I get in. Gone. Just like that. Snap.

A girl is what I am.

OLIVIA *stands in light.*

OLIVIA: I knew. I definitely knew. I was a girl through and through. Boys, they were hard to take. Always in your face. I had no brothers, no male cousins, no boys next door. My dad's one of them gentle men not into macho crap. I wasn't used to boys. They spoiled things, they wrecked games, they broke toys. They were alien, they were other, they were hard core. They were always shooting with imaginary guns or wrestling each other on the floor. They were always right, always first, always wanted more. They pushed and shoved and punched. Always: 'I won!' Always had an excuse: 'I meant to do that'. Always saving face: 'Didn't hurt'. Always faking it: 'Don't give a fuck'.

I didn't find them interesting. I didn't find them funny. I didn't find them cute. I've heard the 'boys will be boys' crap. What is that?

With boys I was shy. They made me want to cry. With no-one else was I like that. They'd come near me and I'd become nervous, tongue-tied, begin to shake. They were too loud, too rough, too angry. I didn't understand them. Not at all.

I've never had one of them as a friend. Not a single male friend. Not one. Someone told me that it wasn't possible because in the end, all all boys want to do is fuck you.

I've had boyfriends. Two. I got my first because I thought I should. Because that's what you're meant to do. Have a boyfriend. Just the one with whom you spend most of your time. It was an accident, my first boyfriend. I was sixteen and I thought I was running out of time. He was the brother of a friend of mine. I thought he'll do. It was hard to think of things to talk about. Watching hundreds of downloaded films saved us from that. Never kissed, never pecked each other's cheek, never felt inclined. I don't remember what happened. We just stopped one day, and thank god, never saw each other again.

My second relationship was a more serious one. We talked. We had sex. We went out, had fun. I met his dad and mum. I thought we were going well. Suddenly he moves on, to someone else, someone who wants to have sex with him a lot, who is passionate, he says. Amazing in bed, he says. Clearly I'm not. I'm not. I've tried a few things. I've laid there, breathing big and groaning loud and whispering shit like, fuck me, fuck me hard. Faking it in the effort that somehow I could make it real, and I'd really feel, something intense, pleasure, feel intense pleasure. It would be good to feel that. Once, when I was faking it, groaning loudly and writhing about, he asked me what I was doing. Can you stop? It's putting me off.

I never feel completely at ease, never allow myself to get carried away or lose myself, or do as I please. I don't give in to the pleasure. Never. I like sex but I like the idea of it so much better. On my own I have no problem whatsoever.

I'd like to be in love. To give it a crack. To feel excited when I see someone, to feel over the moon, feel my temperature rise at his touch. I'd like that. Look into someone's eyes and stay there looking for the longest time. Run into someone's arms and be swept away. To say stuff like, you're the best thing in my life. You're the man of my dreams. You and I, we're a perfect match. It's cliché I know but what's wrong with that? And talk about important things too, tell each other secrets, painful things, things we've never revealed to anyone else. And give each other advice. I might say, don't do that, that would be an awful mistake to do that, and he'd say, you're right, thanks for that. Shit like that.

I'd like to have good sex like tender sex or loving sex, sometimes passionate, sometimes put-you-to-sleep sex. Nothing try-hard, simple, loving, sweet sex. Give it some time so it can last the distance and get past the awkward stuff. I'd like that.

For a while I stopped looking. Got sick of it. Got sick of feeling there was something wrong with me. Poor bugger me wondering why no-one wants me. Not good enough, pretty enough, sexy enough, just not enough. Got sick of myself and wondering how I came to this. How come? How come I'm consumed by loving someone? Wanting someone, wanting wanting wanting someone who hopefully wants me back. I thought I'd never be a woman like that.

Used to think I might travel, see things, go to extraordinary places, like that woman who rode camels across the desert, or the one who sailed a yacht around the world. Thought I might climb a mountain, canoe down rapids, work on trawlers far out at sea. But I knew that was never going to be me. Those dreams frightened me. I would do none of those things alone. Too scared.

What of? Men, I guess.

RUBY *stands in light.*

RUBY: I knew. I knew for sure. I always knew I wasn't one of them. I envied them. I don't remember ever not envying them. I wanted what they had, I wanted the rough and I wanted the tumble and I wanted tough, to rumble, to run fast, climb too high, to be first, all covered in dirt. I wanted to yell at the top of my voice, and curse, tell everyone, no, I'm not doing that, no, I'm not coming in and no, I'm not getting down.

I didn't want to do what I was told, I wanted to be bold. And funny. And rude. Eat as much as I liked. Eat like a pig. Let the juice of a hamburger spill down my chin. I wanted to be the one told to get out of the class. I wanted to say, fuck you and piss off and don't fucking tell me what to do. Naughty. Really naughty. I love all that.

I was trussed up, stitched in tight. I was stockings and patent leather shoes. I was flounced and frilled and bows and lace. I was dresses and skirts and mind the dirt. Stains on a blouse, a torn hem, a lost button were met with tut-tutts and sighs. Too much movement drew a sudden slap on the thigh. Don't run, watch out, not so fast, slow down, careful, careful, careful, quieten down, that's not nice, close your legs, don't shout, listen, be quiet, watch your mouth, be good, a good girl, a good good girl, sit still, smile.

While all the boys run wild.

I learnt things in my teens. I learnt how to make boys like me. I learnt how to make myself seem like some glittering prize. I laid on make-up thick and coloured my eyelids and lips, I powdered and preened and plucked and shaved and painted my skin. I learnt a whole lot of feminine wiles, coquettish smiles, licks of the tongue across the lips, bras that gave an extra lift. I learned how to perform; I became skilled in the art of drawing them in.

First make the eye contact intense. But playful at the same time. Arch an eyebrow, smile the slightest smile, then the tongue across the lips thing. Drives them wild. Hilarious. Allow the legs to slightly splay. Ridiculous. Maybe laugh now. Not too loud. You're fun, you know what's going on, you're full of promise, full of suggestion, and you'll follow through, no question. Might move the body so, as if it's imagining, feeling him against your skin, feels good, fits nice. Hold off on the kiss. Don't give it away. Move in close, bring him to you and move away. Teasing. An art, I tell you. Lovely, lovely flirting. But got to be careful; too slutty can turn them away or encourage rough play.

Earlier on I got myself into a bit of trouble, reeled them in before I knew what to do with them. I'm sixteen. Putting myself out there, on display, strutting my stuff, giving the performance of a lifetime, at some club I shouldn't have been allowed in. I draw the attention of some guy much older than me, a cruel-mouthed man with eyes that had me in his sights. I have the feeling I'm not in for a good night. I try to dance around him, to find a way out, but he has me pinned. Like I belong to him. He buys me drink after drink and I can't remember a thing until I wake up in some shitty hotel room. I let him finish off and when he falls asleep, I leave. How could I put myself in such a stupid position? How could I drink so much that I can no longer control the situation? And I worried I'd damaged myself because I still had a tampon in?

Now I sit on one vodka lime and soda the entire night. And I choose; no cruel-mouthed bastards, thank you. No line-ups, no queues, I never put myself in a group situation no matter how hard they beg. If someone wants to have sex with me he comes home or we get a hotel room alone.

 She looks at her mobile.

Look at these. Dicks. Dicks. And more dicks. They send them to me all the time. Erect. Of course. Like little boys saying, have a look how big this is. And look at the texts: 'Suck this.' 'Blow this.' 'Choke on this.'

I've only got a certain amount of time, a window of opportunity before I'll no longer be able to participate, when I won't have what it takes to bring them in. When this is gone to flab. When there's only so much the make-up can cover, the push-up bra and invisible tape can fake. I might buy some time if I got a few tucks and lifts and some bigger tits to keep them thinking, I'd still like a piece of her.

One day, I suppose, I'll marry someone. Maybe. Not one of these young bucks. Probably someone with a gut, a bald patch, and short. Someone I love, I guess. I don't mind because I will always look back and know I've had the best.

I'm up for the sex. I love it. I want it. I want it as much as anyone. I want it with strong, gorgeous young men. And I found a club with lots of them. When they enter the room it's like royalty has walked in. Footballers most of them. Come to relax after a hard game, come to let their hair down, come to drink, to snort a line, come to fuck their brains out.

And here I am!

The three WOMEN *enter the club to a show of moving lights and loud, pulsating music. They check out the scene.*

The music swells and entices three MEN *out onto the dance floor.*

They howl. They dance. They give it their all. Powerful, suggestive, lewd at times, and sometimes comical.

They overlap, repeat each other's sentences and sometimes speak as one.

MEN: Have a look at that.
    And that.
    And that.
    Oh my god, and what about that?
    Let me get my hands on that.
    Let me get my hands on that.
    Hey hey hey.
    Oh, yes yes yes.
    Ah-huh, ah-huh.
    Ah-huh.
    Babes galore.
    Babes.
    Chick-a-dees.

Ladies.
Not bad.
Not bad.
Not bad at all.
Gorgeous.
Sublime.
Sublime?
Absolutely divine.
Divine.
Let me get my hands on that.
Let me get my hands on that.
Let me get my hands on that.
And that.
And…
That.
Look at her.
Look at her.
Beautiful.
She's mine.
She's mine.
I don't think so. She's mine.
Mine.
You're drooling.
I am.
Settle.
Settle.
Settle.
Don't give her too much.
Just enough.
Enough.
Have a look at her.
Oh my god.
Have a look at those thighs.
Oh me, oh my.
At those tits.
Have a look at the arse on her.
Feel my heartbeat.

Sweet.
Mmm.
Mmm.
Mmm.
Love her.
Love her.
She's mine.

The three MEN *holler for* RUBY*'s attention.*

Ruby!
Ruby!
Ruby!

    RUBY *ignores them.*

Hey Ruby!
Hey Ruby!
Hey Ruby!

    RUBY *playfully deigns to acknowledge them.*

RUBY: Oh, it's me you're calling? It's me you want? It's me you're desperate for? What!?
MEN: Looking good, Ruby.
RUBY: Thank you.
MEN: Looking great.
RUBY: Thank you.
MEN: Looking fine.
RUBY: And again.
MEN: In good shape.
RUBY: What can I say?
MEN: In great shape.
RUBY: A girl's got to keep fit.
MEN: Trim, taught and…
RUBY: Terrific. I know.
MEN: You in training, Ruby?
RUBY: Got to keep in good nick.
MEN: Pumping iron?
RUBY: Flexibility is key.

MEN: Looking strong.
RUBY: As an ox.
MEN: Looking like you could take us on.
RUBY: Try me.
MEN: Reckon you'd last the distance?
RUBY: I'll be there at the finish line.
MEN: Got the stamina, you reckon?
RUBY: Wear you out anytime.

The MEN *hoot in delight.*

The three MEN *split and come together in a huddle.*
ANNIE *fixates on one of them.*

ANNIE: Sean! Sean! Sean!

The MEN *ignore her.*

Hey, Sean! Hey, Sean! Hey, Sean!

ANNIE *persists.*

It's me, Annie. Sean? It's me. It's me. It's Annie.

Two of the MEN *form a barrier between* ANNIE *and* SEAN.

MAN 1: Piss off, Annie.
MAN 2: Piss off.

She tries to get around them and they frustrate her every move.

ANNIE: Sean, it's me. It's Annie. It's Annie.

SEAN *steps through the others and takes* ANNIE *by the elbow and leads her away. He gives her no chance to respond.*

SEAN: What are you doing, Annie? We've been through this. We've talked about it. We came to the decision that you'd stop. You said you'd stop. You said you wouldn't do it anymore, that you'd give it a rest. Do you remember, Annie, do you remember? You promised me you'd stop.
ANNIE: Have you missed me?
SEAN: Jesus Christ, stop. Stop!

The other MEN *swoop in and move him away.*

OLIVIA *meets* ANGUS.

He goes to pass, she goes to pass, and they block each other—a familiar routine.

ANGUS: Hi.
OLIVIA: Hi.

At a loss for words they repeat the routine.

Let's try it again. Hi.
ANGUS: Okay. Hi.
OLIVIA: Hi.
ANGUS: Hi. How are you?
OLIVIA: I'm fine. And you?
ANGUS: Pretty good now I've met someone as sexy as you.
OLIVIA: Oh no.

She goes to pass.

ANGUS: Hold on, hold on.
OLIVIA: I don't think so.
ANGUS: I know, I know that was bad.
OLIVIA: So bad.
ANGUS: Help me out with this.
OLIVIA: Okay. You say, how are you?
ANGUS: How are you?
OLIVIA: I'm fine. And you? And you say…
ANGUS: Pretty good now I've … I say, pretty good.
OLIVIA: Yeah, that's good.
ANGUS: Yeah, much better.
OLIVIA: And I say, what's your name?
ANGUS: Angus.
OLIVIA: Nice to meet you, Angus.
ANGUS: You too.

Pause.

OLIVIA: And you say …
ANGUS: Shit! What? What do I say?
OLIVIA: Oh my god, you ask me what's mine.
ANGUS: Oh my god, I know that. What's your name?
OLIVIA: Olivia.

ANGUS: Olivia. That's a lovely name.
OLIVIA: Thanks.
ANGUS: This is going well.
OLIVIA: Mmmmm.
ANGUS: Wait, wait, give it a go. We'll warm up. We will, I know. We will. And you say…
OLIVIA: We will.

Pause.

ANGUS: Okay. What do you do?
OLIVIA: I'm doing an arts degree.
ANGUS: And what will that make you?
OLIVIA: A teacher maybe. At a secondary school. What about you?
ANGUS: I play footy.
OLIVIA: I mean what job do you do?
ANGUS: That's it. I'm a footballer. I play in the league.
OLIVIA: Oh-oh.
ANGUS: What?
OLIVIA: This is not good.
ANGUS: Forget it. I'm a doctor. I'm a GP.
OLIVIA: You're really a footballer?
ANGUS: I am.
OLIVIA: A professional footballer?
ANGUS: You don't know anything about footy, do you?
OLIVIA: No.
ANGUS: Do you go?
OLIVIA: No.
ANGUS: You don't barrack for a team?
OLIVIA: No.
ANGUS: You've never watched a game?
OLIVIA: Seen a bit on tele.
ANGUS: You don't like footy?
OLIVIA: No.
ANGUS: You don't like footy?
OLIVIA: No.
ANGUS: You don't like footy?
OLIVIA: No!
ANGUS: Oh-oh.

OLIVIA: I know. What will we do now?
ANGUS: We're in too deep now.
OLIVIA: You reckon?
ANGUS: Way over our heads.
OLIVIA: We could try to walk on.

They try but get in each other's way.

ANGUS: Told you.
OLIVIA: Shit!
ANGUS: We're stuck with each other.
OLIVIA: What are we going to talk about?
ANGUS: I don't know.
OLIVIA: This is bad.
ANGUS: It's shocking.
OLIVIA: It is.
ANGUS and OLIVIA: [*simultaneously*] Want a drink?
ANGUS and OLIVIA: [*simultaneously*] Good idea.

RUBY *and* JAMES *sit at the bar together.*

JAMES: What about him?
RUBY: Yes.
JAMES: Him?
RUBY: Yes.
JAMES: Him?
RUBY: Ah-huh.
JAMES: Him?
RUBY: Yep.
JAMES: Far out. Him?
RUBY: Yep.
JAMES: Him?
RUBY: I think so.

He points.

Yes. Yes. Yes. Yes. Yes. Aaah—yes. Kind of.
JAMES: Kind of?
RUBY: He was drunk.
JAMES: What about that one by the door?

RUBY: Yes.
JAMES: Really?
RUBY: Yes, really. Quite a few times.
JAMES: A few times?
RUBY: Quite a few times.
JAMES: I'm surprised.
RUBY: Why?
JAMES: He's not your sort.
RUBY: My sort. He's exactly my sort.
JAMES: He's not pretty.
RUBY: He's gorgeous.
JAMES: No, he's not.
RUBY: Look at his body.
JAMES: What about me?
RUBY: What about you?
JAMES: Am I your sort?
RUBY: Yes! Of course.

He smiles.

What? What?

JAMES: Nothing. I'm glad, that's all. Is there anyone here you haven't slept with?
RUBY: What are you insinuating, James? Him. Him. Him. And him over there. And that group there.
JAMES: I was the best, wasn't I?
RUBY: For sure.
JAMES: No, really. I was very good.
RUBY: You were excellent.

He smiles.

JAMES: Really?
RUBY: Really.
JAMES: So…
RUBY: That's enough now.

ANNIE *attaches herself to* SEAN *and the* MEN. *When they move, she follows. They change directions and she sticks with them. They turn on her.*

SEAN: What are you doing, Annie?
MEN: What are you doing?
   What are you doing, Annie?
   Give it a rest.
   You're being a pest.
   Yeah, a pest.
   Enough.
   Enough's enough.
   You're driving us nuts.

   They move on and again ANNIE *attaches herself.*

   And again, they turn on her.

SEAN: What are you doing, Annie?
MEN: What the hell.
   What is this?
SEAN: Come on, Annie, give it a miss.

   They move on, ANNIE *doggedly with them.*

MEN: Go away!
   Piss off!
   On your way!

   Two of the MEN *turn on* SEAN.

   Do something, would you?
SEAN: What am I meant to do?
MEN: Tell her to piss off.
SEAN: I've told her.
MEN: Tell her she's past her use-by date.
SEAN: I've told her.
MEN: Tell her she's a crazy slut.
SEAN: I've told her. I've told her a hundred times.
MEN: Tell her again.

   SEAN *takes* ANNIE *aside.*

SEAN: Listen, Annie, listen to me, listen to what I'm saying to you. I feel for you, I really do, but it's got to stop. You've got to go home. Are you listening to me? Are you? Because this is over the top. I don't know what you want but whatever it is it's too much. You've got to go home. There's nothing here for you.

He backs away.

You got it? Got it, Annie?

He returns to the others and they move off. ANNIE *follows.*

They groan. Each of them attempts to discourage her.

MEN: You're embarrassing yourself.
Making a fool of yourself.
You're a nutcase.
We've tried being nice.
Tried not to hurt your feelings.
To make you feel bad.
But time's up.
We're out of patience.
All used up.
Leave us alone.
Go home.
You're harassing us.
You are.
Leave us alone.
Give it up.
Forget us.
There's nothing here for you.
You've got to go.
Go on, get out.
Do you hear us?
Annie?
Do you hear us?
Do you?
Fuck off!

ANNIE stays resolute.

They groan.

OLIVIA *and* ANGUS *at the bar.*

ANGUS: Have you ever wanted something so much that you knew some part of you would die if it didn't come off?
OLIVIA: I don't think I've ever wanted anything that much.

ANGUS: Wanting so hard, so hard that you know there's a danger something might crack?
OLIVIA: I wish I had a little bit of that.
ANGUS: Leaving yourself wide open because there's nothing else. If you fail there's nothing at all that can take its place.
OLIVIA: I'd like to want more.
ANGUS: I'm sitting at the table eating toast, out with friends, celebrating my kid sister's birthday, seeing a film, taking a walk, in the pool swimming laps, in the middle of a conversation but I'm not there. I'm in the game, in the play, taking a mark, kicking a goal, tackling an opponent to the ground. There's something truly mad about it. Have you ever felt mad for something? Mad as a cut snake?
OLIVIA: I've liked doing stuff. Liked. That's about it.
ANGUS: It's like you're sick with it, in pain, got some disease and there's nothing can be done.
OLIVIA: Shit!
ANGUS: It's infected every part of you. It's eaten into your brain.
OLIVIA: Oh, my god.
ANGUS: It's extreme, I know, it's over the top. And when the dream comes true and you get selected the sickness gets worse.
OLIVIA: I've never felt that. I wish I did. I want that. To feel that.
ANGUS: Got to be the best. Mentally, physically and emotionally in sync, in control, at the top of every contest. Take on the fiercest situations. In top form, in the play as it hurtles along at a frenzied pace. Work on instinct, never second guess, never hesitate while the stadium rocks and the crowd booms and adrenalin pumps. They're hollering and hooting and calling out my name or hissing and booing and telling me I ought to be ashamed.
OLIVIA: That's too mean. I couldn't do it. I couldn't withstand that kind of exposure.
ANGUS: The team saves you. It's the team you're working your guts out for. It's the team you're risking your life for. It's the team that you put your neck on the line for.
OLIVIA: Now you've lost me for sure.
ANGUS: There's nothing we wouldn't do for one another. Nothing we don't know about each other. We've seen each other down in the pits, seen each other lose it, seen each other soar, and come down with lips

split, with eyes bruised and noses smashed. Seen each other carried off with bones broken and heads cracked and backs strapped. Seen the misery of our mates told that it's their last game, they'll never play again. Seen the dream spent. In a moment. In a heartbeat. Spent.

Silence.

Oh, shit! I forgot. You don't like footy. And I'm talking footy and I've bored you to death. Prattling on, not drawing breath. You don't like footy. Are you sure about that? You're really sure you don't like it? Just a bit? No. Don't look at me like that. Give me a chance. Here we go. Tell me about your life. How many kids in your family? Where do you come? I bet you're the first. Are you the first? Do you live at home? With your mum and dad? Are you enjoying yourself? Having a good night? Loving the company? He's great, isn't he? That guy you're hanging with. Quite a catch.

Two MEN *exuberantly flank* ANGUS.

MEN: Angus!
 Angus!
 We were wondering where you'd got to.
 Where you were hiding.
ANGUS: From you bastards. And now you've found me.
MEN: And now we know why.
 Now we know what you're up to.
 Who's this you've been keeping secret?
 Who's this you've been keeping to yourself all this time?
ANGUS: Olivia, meet a couple of team mates of mine.
MEN: Olivia?
 Olivia. Lovely to meet you.
 Where the hell did you find her?
 You're a sly dog, Angus, that's what you are.
 She's gorgeous.
 She is.
 Beautiful.
 She is.
 What the hell she doing with you, mate?
 Too good for you, mate.
 Way out of your league.

It's a waste.
It is.
ANGUS: Piss off, please.
MEN: Olivia, you can do better than this guy.
Much better.
There's me for example.
And me.
You decide.
ANGUS: Piss off.
MEN: Is he giving you a hard time?
Is that it?
Is he cramping your style?
He's known to be a bit hard line.
Don't let him stop you from enjoying yourself.
Don't feel stuck with this dick.
If you want us to get rid of him.
If you need us to tell him to get lost.
To send him on his way.
Have him chucked out.
Just say the word.
It's okay.
We'll tell him …
Back off, Angus.
You heard.
She's not interested, mate.
Give the girl some space.

> *They playfully escort* OLIVIA *aside.*
>
> *They move in close.*

Now, Olivia, if you'd like to have a good time.
A really good time.
Quality time.
The very best.
Look no further.
We're here.
Put it to the test.
Happy to oblige.

ANGUS *comes to her rescue.*

ANGUS: Goodbye. Have a good night.

He whisks her away.

OLIVIA: Oh, my god!

ANGUS: They're a bit pissed, fooling around. They're not that bad. You have to meet them another time. They're great blokes. They are.

ANNIE *dances to a love song. The dance evolves slowly into a mockery of sexual desire; a parody. It's vulgar. It's edgy. And vulnerable. She pushes the sexy stuff far.*

For some time SEAN *and the chorus of* MEN *watch on. Angry. And* ANNIE *fades away.*

MEN: Oh, my god.
  What the fuck.
  Have a look at that.
  Full-on.
  Over the top.
  Out of control.
  Someone's got to do something.
  What?
  Got to set her right.
  How?
  Kick her out.
  Put her in a fucking nuthouse.
  What are we meant to do, that's what I'd like to know?
  How are we meant to react?
  How are we meant to deal with girls like that?
  I'm in the street, in the supermarket, driving my car, and they see me, recognise me instantly and they scream, blow me kisses, mouth 'fuck me'. It happens to me constantly.
  We can have anyone we want.
  But careful of jail bait.
  In bedrooms, in bathrooms, in closets, in alleys, in cars, in lifts, on top of bars, I've fucked my brains out.
  After a game, win or lose, I'm pumped. The blood surges through my veins and I'm on the hunt.

A wild man, a crazy man, a man looking for blood, looking for cunt.
A hard and quick fuck, it's all we want.
And it's laid on.
At our beck and call.
They're willing.
So willing.
Shit, you have no idea how willing they are.
In a taxi, in a park, in a fancy restaurant while I'm eating my cock's being sucked.
Against a wall, in the surf, in the cinema, in the toilet with my best friend's wife.
You get to thinking, this is the life.
This is what it's all about.
Riding high.
Top of the world.
Invincible.
Like a god maybe, a Roman one, with a breastplate and a leather skirt.
And we're told to rein it in.
To show restraint.
To behave ourselves.
To be nice.
To treat them right.
Show some respect.
We're told, be careful.
Don't be fooled.
Don't be enticed.
Don't be sucked in.
They're bad news, these girls.
Want to make trouble, these girls.
Want to burst our bubble, these girls.
They're conniving, they're spiteful, nothing but malicious bitches setting a trap.
Don't fall into it.
Don't get snagged.
Don't get bit.
We're told to keep a lid on it.

Use your common sense, they say.
Walk away.
Walk away.
Walk away.
Yeah right.
Yeah right.
Yeah right.
They follow.
They follow.
They fucking follow!
They track us down.
They park their cars outside our homes.
They constantly text us.
They don't give up.
They beg us.
They're desperate for us.
Shit, you have no idea how much.
They want us.
They want us.
They want us.
They want us some more.
With them there's no holding back.
No stopping them.
There's not.
They want us.
They want us.
They want us.
They want us some more.
It's overwhelming.
It is.
It's frightening.
It is.
It's terrifying.
It is.

Women's toilets.
ANNIE, RUBY *and* OLIVIA *stand at the mirror, applying lipstick.*

RUBY: Can I give you some advice?

Silence.

It's none of my business.

Silence.

You can tell me to keep my trap shut.

ANNIE: Are you talking to me?

RUBY: There's something I think you should know.

ANNIE: What?

RUBY: You're going at it too hard.

ANNIE: I'm what?

RUBY: You're overdoing it.

ANNIE: Overdoing what?

RUBY: You're pushing it.

ANNIE: What am I pushing?

RUBY: You're shoving it down their necks.

ANNIE: I'm shoving it down their necks. What is it exactly that I'm shoving?

RUBY: Sex.

ANNIE: Oh, it's sex I'm pushing and shoving.

RUBY: It's too much.

ANNIE: You're right, it's none of your business.

OLIVIA: I think it's a bit much too.

ANNIE: Oh, here we go, there's someone else who wants to have a say about what I do.

RUBY: I think you should go home.

ANNIE: What?!

RUBY: Go home.

ANNIE: Why would I do that?

RUBY: Because what you're doing is over the top. Way over the top. It's giving me the shits.

OLIVIA: It's not safe.

ANNIE: What are you talking about?

OLIVIA: What you're doing, it's not safe.

ANNIE: What am I doing?

RUBY: You're asking for trouble.

ANNIE: I like trouble.

RUBY: You're out of control.
ANNIE: I know exactly what I'm doing.
OLIVIA: I don't think you do.
ANNIE: It's got nothing to do with either of you.
RUBY: That's not true.
OLIVIA: It has a lot to with us.
ANNIE: What I do is what I do.
RUBY: You make it hard for us.
ANNIE: What?!
OLIVIA: You put us at risk.
RUBY: You make it dangerous.
OLIVIA: For all of us.
ANNIE: Oh shit, I never knew. I'm making the world unsafe. Me. I'm making it a scary place. I'm doing that. Give me a break.
RUBY: You're offering yourself up like on a plate.
ANNIE: [*calling mockingly*] Hey, boys, here I am!
RUBY: Go home, would you, for fuck's sake.
OLIVIA: We're actually trying to look after you.
ANNIE: I don't need looking after.
RUBY: Believe me, you do.
OLIVIA: You do.
ANNIE: I'm a big girl. I can look after myself.
RUBY: That's not what it looks like to me.
OLIVIA: You look vulnerable.
ANNIE: I'm way past vulnerable.
RUBY: You're like a scared little girl.
ANNIE: I don't get scared.
RUBY: You should.
ANNIE: Tough as nails, that's me.
OLIVIA: You don't see yourself.
ANNIE: I see myself perfectly.
RUBY: You don't know the message you put out.
ANNIE: What message is that?
OLIVIA: They look at you and they see someone they can do anything to.
RUBY: You're like a fucking doormat.
OLIVIA: The message then is that's true for us all.
RUBY: They can do anything they want to any of us.

Voices, male, call out: 'Ruby.' 'Ruby.' 'Ruby.'

RUBY *stands alone, swaying gently with the music, and waves to acknowledge each call.*

JAMES *enters.*

JAMES: What?!
RUBY: What?
JAMES: You're not hooked up.
RUBY: Not yet, I'm not.
JAMES: Not a one sniffing about.
RUBY: Not yet.
JAMES: Not one.
RUBY: The night's not over yet.
JAMES: No takers.
RUBY: Plenty. Choosy is what I am.
JAMES: Choosy? You?
RUBY: Yes, James, I am. I once chose you.
JAMES: That's true. Where are they, Ruby?
RUBY: They'll come. They always do.
JAMES: Oh god, Ruby, you're not losing your touch?
RUBY: No, James, I'm not.
JAMES: Just saying, wondering if your time's up.
RUBY: You know, I don't think I like you much.
JAMES: You love me.
RUBY: No, I don't
JAMES: You're just not ready to admit it yet.
RUBY: Oh, that must be it.
JAMES: Think about it.
RUBY: I don't need to.
JAMES: Give it a moment to sink in.
RUBY: Off you go now, you're cramping my style.
JAMES: I'm here ready to step up.
RUBY: You're taking up way too much space.
JAMES: You can rely on me, you know that.
RUBY: I swear, it's you, you're putting them off.
JAMES: I'm utterly faithful, loyal through and through. True.
RUBY: James, why don't you fuck off?

JAMES: Remember there's always me if you have no luck.
RUBY: James! Go!
JAMES: Here I am waiting for you.
RUBY: Go away!
JAMES: Okay. Okay. I'm serious, you know?
RUBY: Now!
JAMES: I'm going.
RUBY: Far away.
JAMES: How far?

> *She gestures.*
>
> *He drags it out.*

RUBY: Far. Far. Far.

SEAN *stands alone.*

ANNIE *appears behind him.*

ANNIE: I am not someone you can suddenly dump. I am not garbage you put out in the street. I am not the something you forgot, someone you blot out. I'm not done and dusted, a name you scribble out. An old rag, leftovers on a plate, on the nose, not a, go on, away you go, nothing here for you, fuck off, I wipe my hands of you. That's not me. It's not. Got to get something, take something, make something, get a bit of me back. You think you can ignore me? I don't think so. You think I'll go away? Uh-uh. You think I'll give up? No way. That I'll become unstuck? I'm sticking. Dug my nails in. Can you feel them? I'm here to stay.

> SEAN *turns to confront her. She's gone.*

At the bar. OLIVIA *and* ANGUS *sing along to a very popular love song.*

ANGUS: Have you ever been in love?
OLIVIA: I don't think so. Have you?
ANGUS: Yes.
OLIVIA: Really in love?
ANGUS: Of course I have.
OLIVIA: Who with?
ANGUS: Miss Tsourakis.

OLIVIA: Who's she?
ANGUS: A teacher I had.

    OLIVIA *scoffs*.

I loved her. I loved her so much. For years I loved her.
OLIVIA: What happened?
ANGUS: When I was about fourteen, I stopped.
OLIVIA: Anyone else?
ANGUS: Not really. Not yet.
OLIVIA: I'm not sure about this love stuff.
ANGUS: You don't believe in love?
OLIVIA: I do. I think I do. I'm not sure I do.
ANGUS: You don't believe in love?
OLIVIA: Maybe not.
ANGUS: You don't believe in love?
OLIVIA: I want to, I really do.
ANGUS: You don't…
OLIVIA: I think it might be a load of crap.
ANGUS: God! Love's not a load of crap. Love's …
OLIVIA: What?
ANGUS: If you don't believe in love, you don't believe in anything. Got to believe in love.
OLIVIA: You believe you'll meet someone one day, and you'll go, and she'll go, you are for me and I am for you, no doubt, we are made for one another and it will never wear out and we will be together forever and ever. You believe that?
ANGUS: Yes, I believe that.
OLIVIA: You really believe that?

    He sings a refrain from the love song.

I want to believe that too.
ANGUS: I say, here's to love.

    He raises his glass.

And you say …
OLIVIA: Here's to love.

    They clink and drink.

I don't believe it.

ANGUS: That's just wrong.
OLIVIA: Is it?
ANGUS: You shouldn't be here.
OLIVIA: What?
ANGUS: You should be at home. On your own.
OLIVIA: Why should I?
ANGUS: Because everyone here is looking for love.
OLIVIA: Believe me, they're not.
ANGUS: You're wasting everyone's time.
OLIVIA: I'm willing to be proved wrong.
ANGUS: Let's drink to that.

They clink glasses and drink.

You never know when it might happen to you.
OLIVIA: I don't think it's ever going to happen to me.
ANGUS: It might sneak up on you.
OLIVIA: You make it sound like a stalker.
ANGUS: It might be just around the corner. It might be about to jump out and surprise you and you won't have a clue.

They look at each other for a while, and smile.

OLIVIA: Okay okay, I take it back. I'm ready for it. Love. Come on. Come my way. And you say…
ANGUS: Let's drink to that.

ANNIE *stands alone.*

SEAN *suddenly appears behind her.*

SEAN: This is what the world feels when one of you comes up against one of us. They feel a great regret, they feel any accusation against us must be suspect. They feel a kind of grief, visceral-like, in their gut. This young man might lose it all. And what's he done? He's made a mistake. He's young, a bit foolish, a bit careless. He had too much to drink. Forgive him, for Christ's sake! Give him a warning. Tell him to watch his step. There's no way he meant to do the things you suggest. The world can't bear to witness him throwing it all away. They won't allow it. He's in his prime, this young man, a wonderful athlete, at the top of his game. Their hearts are with him. He lifts their spirits high. He soars and they soar with him. They won't let him fall. Not for the likes of you, a stupid, flirtatious girl, who was asking for it, who knew what she was doing, was up for it, whose only intent is to bring this fine footballer down and ruin his career. The world aches at the thought of us dealing with the likes of you.

ANNIE *turns to confront him. He's gone.*

Towards the end of the night.
RUBY *dances alone, slow and lovely.*
JAMES *watches for a while and finally joins her until the music ends.*

JAMES: You look sad.
RUBY: Sad? I'm not sad.
JAMES: A bit sad.
RUBY: How am I sad?
JAMES: Look at you.
RUBY: Oh my god, James, I'm not sad!
JAMES: It's what you look like, dancing all alone …
RUBY: I've danced on my own before, James.
JAMES: … at the end of the night.
RUBY: I've gone home on my own before, James.
JAMES: Come on, you've got to admit it, it's sad, just a bit, you, week in week out, on the prowl.
RUBY: Oh, you think that's sad?
JAMES: Hanging out. Looking to score.
RUBY: It's not sad.
JAMES: It's fucking sad. Tragic even.
RUBY: Tragic. Fuck me.
JAMES: What's it about? What do you get? Where's the sense in it?
RUBY: It's no big secret, James. It's about sex.
JAMES: That's all they want.
RUBY: That's all I want.
JAMES: That's it?
RUBY: That's it.
JAMES: They're using you, you know that?
RUBY: I'm using them, you know that?
JAMES: I used you.

RUBY: I used you.
JAMES: You have no idea what they call you.
RUBY: What do they call me?
JAMES: The things they say about you.
RUBY: What do they say about me?
JAMES: It's not hard to guess.
RUBY: What the hell, James, give it a rest! I want sex. I like sex. What's wrong with that?
JAMES: You don't get it.
RUBY: What's there to get?
JAMES: You could have so much more.
RUBY: I don't want more.
JAMES: I don't believe you. We all want more than that.
RUBY: You think I should give this up. You think I should settle down. You think I should be with one man, have a kid or two, that there's something not right about what I do.
JAMES: What about love? Is there anything wrong with that?
RUBY: No, nothing at all, but what I want is sex. Sex. Sex, James, sex. You think there's something unseemly about that.
JAMES: It's a bit sad, that's all.
RUBY: If I tell you that this is what I want then I'm sad because I don't want more. If I tell you, I want sex and that's all I want then I'm sad because sex is something I shouldn't want. If I tell you that I'm queen of this, you'll call me tragic, you'll think I'm a deluded fool. Whatever I say to you, if I say, I run my own ship, it's too sad. I'm sad you think. Must be. Sad. But, James, I'm not.
JAMES: I'm offering you something.
RUBY: No thanks.
JAMES: You don't know a good offer when it stares you in the face. You are fucking sad.
RUBY: What about you?
JAMES: What about me?
RUBY: Are you sad?
JAMES: Why would I be sad?
RUBY: Losing your touch.
JAMES: What?
RUBY: Body's tired, not keeping up. A bit worn out.
JAMES: Fuck.

RUBY: Not playing so much. Besieged by injury after injury.
JAMES: Been a bit tough.
RUBY: Losing the spark. Not quite able to hit the mark.
JAMES: Something like that.
RUBY: Last season perhaps?
JAMES: Perhaps.
RUBY: Bit sad. Like me, I guess.
JAMES: I guess.
RUBY: Yes.

>JAMES *is about to leave.*

JAMES: Someone will come.
RUBY: What?
JAMES: Time's getting on, there'll be someone for sure.
RUBY: For sure.
JAMES: Someone who's left their run too late. The pretty young things all taken. And you'll be here and he'll be happy because here's Ruby. Ruby! Ruby's here waiting.

SEAN *and the* MEN *dump* ANNIE *out the door.*
She immediately struggles to re-enter.
They dump her again.

MEN: Go home!
   Go home!
   Go the fuck home!
   Don't you dare come back in.
   We're warning you, Annie.
   Go on.
   Go.
   Take off.
   We don't want to see you again.
ANNIE: Let me in.
MEN: No way.
ANNIE: Let me in.
MEN: Not on your life.
   You're done.
   Off you go.

ANNIE: You've got no right.
MEN: You're a limpet, Annie.
   A leech.
   You suck us dry.
   We don't know what else to do with you.
   We've tried.
   We have to put you out.
   To be free of you.
SEAN: I tried to explain to you that there was nothing in it, there was nowhere for it to go. You came round and we slept together and it was fun. It was good, I thought. For me and for you. It was fine, I thought. You were cool. I thought you knew what was going on. You acted as if you knew. What am I meant to do?
MEN: What are we meant to do?
SEAN: I tried to explain. Over and over, I explained. It was a bit of fun. That's all.
MEN: A bit of fun.
SEAN: That's all.
MEN: And you came round.
ANNIE: I did.
MEN: And you came round.
ANNIE: I did.
MEN: And you came round.
ANNIE: I did.
MEN: We all knew what for.
ANNIE: I'm not sure.
MEN: You came round.
   Wouldn't leave us alone.
   You came.
ANNIE: Wanting something.
MEN: You came.
   Hysterical.
   You came.
   Calling us names.
   The names you called us.
   You came.
   Angry.

ANNIE: Furious.
MEN: Deranged.
   You came.
   Stoned off your head.
   Turning up in our beds.
   Cursing.
   And crying.
ANNIE: About something stolen.
MEN: Stolen from you, you said.
   Now it's come to an end.
   Finished.
   Finally.
   It's got to be.
   Go home, Annie.
   Piss off, Annie.
   And don't come back.

Towards the end of the night.

OLIVIA *and* ANGUS *have had a few.*

OLIVIA: What now?
ANGUS: I don't know.
OLIVIA: No, no, no. You say, shall we say 'bye 'bye, or will we kick on?
ANGUS: And you say, let's / kick on.
OLIVIA: / Kick on. Yeah? Will we?
ANGUS: For sure.
OLIVIA: I'm not ready to let you go. And you say …
ANGUS: … I don't want you to.
OLIVIA: And I say, because I've had a great night and I like you.
ANGUS: And I like you.
OLIVIA: What'll we do?
ANGUS: More dancing?
OLIVIA: There's no music.
ANGUS: Listen. Can't you hear it?

   They dance. Lovely. Charged.

   They stop and look at one another for a while.

  You've got a knockout smile.

OLIVIA: So have you. You're lovely.
ANGUS: Lovely?
OLIVIA: I think you're lovely.
ANGUS: You're lovely too. And, oh my god, look at you.
OLIVIA: And look at you.
ANGUS: You have …
OLIVIA: What?
ANGUS: Magnificent lips.
OLIVIA: You have beautiful eyes.
ANGUS: You have beautiful eyes.
OLIVIA: You are amazingly fit.
ANGUS: You have great tits.
OLIVIA: Oh my god, you've blown it.
ANGUS: No, wait, sorry, sorry, that was a mistake.
OLIVIA: It's all gone to shit.
ANGUS: What I meant to say, is you're in great shape.
OLIVIA: Oh, okay, thank you, that's nice of you to say.
ANGUS: My pleasure. And…
OLIVIA: And?
ANGUS: You do have great tits.

OLIVIA flashes her tits.

OLIVIA: I'm starving.
ANGUS: Me too.
OLIVIA: Nothing will be open.
ANGUS: There's a 7-Eleven on the way.
OLIVIA: On the way where?
ANGUS: One of the boys has an apartment not far from here.
OLIVIA: Why are we going there?
ANGUS: To kick on. He's expecting us. It'll be fun.
OLIVIA: I want a pie.
ANGUS: A pie?
OLIVIA: With sauce.
ANGUS: You're on.

SEAN *stares at his mobile.*

SEAN: Annie!

He's out the door where he and the others dumped ANNIE.
She's waiting for him.
He tries to keep down his panic.

What've you done?
ANNIE: Shared some memories.
SEAN: Where did you get these?
ANNIE: Downloaded them from your phone.
SEAN: When?
ANNIE: Years ago.
SEAN: You've shared them with everyone.
ANNIE: The media. The club. Your coach. Our families.
SEAN: Annie, it was so long ago.
ANNIE: I know, I was sixteen.
SEAN: Wanting to make a name for yourself, is that it, Annie?
ANNIE: I guess. I want the fuss. I want them to talk. I want them to point. I want them to say, that's the girl who's taking them on.
SEAN: Not a chance. This'll blow over. It won't last. Nobody'll give a rat's arse.
ANNIE: I won't let up.
SEAN: They'll call you a liar. Deceitful. Full of crap. Money-grubbing.
ANNIE: I've been called worse.
SEAN: They'll say you asked for it, promiscuous they'll call you, nothing but an attention-seeking slut.
ANNIE: They'll say, you were fucking a sixteen-year-old.

SEAN swipes his mobile. Panic setting in.

SEAN: What you got? Me and the boys with our clothes off. You with your tits out and a medal around your neck. You and some of the boys in bed. Boys being boys, mucking around, up to mischief, nothing in it.
ANNIE: I was sixteen.
SEAN: There's no way you can take us on. We're going to come at you big time. No way you can bring us down. We can do whatever we like. We're going to eat you alive. Because we've got each other. We stick together. We're a team. In the club.

SEAN exits.

ANNIE: Am I feeling the slightest tingle in my fingertips? Is that the taste of blood on my lips?

RUBY *is in the street. She wears a coat. Lifts her face to the rain.*

RUBY: Good to be out of there, in the fresh air, feel the raindrops on my skin, try not think about anything. Let it all wash over me.

She tries.

No such luck. What the fuck, James! What the fuck! Look at this. You've got to be kidding, who doesn't want a piece of this? I've got it. I've got it alright. I've got the goods. I've got the spark, got the moves, the lick of the lips. I can still send them wild. Not done yet, Jimmy boy. Not on your life. Got a long way to go, a long, long way that's for sure. What's not to adore? Here we go, take a look at this.

She makes a move.

And this.

Another move.

How about this?

One more.

I know what this can do. There's a lot more to be had I'm telling you.

OLIVIA *and* ANGUS *lie in bed.* ANGUS *sleeps.*

OLIVIA: Oh, my, god. Look at you. Look at me. Who would have thought? I met you only hours ago and here I am in bed with you and I've just had sex with you and I thought I was going to explode and I thought I was going to rocket out through the window and it was good sex, better than good, excellent sex. The best. The best I've had that's for sure.

ANGUS wakes.

He quietly gets up and pulls his trousers on.

Where are you going?

He leans down and they kiss.

ANGUS: I won't be long.

He leaves.

OLIVIA: Try not to get ahead of yourself, try not to get your hopes up, try not to get all intense. Don't get weird and think there's something more in this than there is. Something really big. Maybe immense. Keep your common sense! Try to be sane, to be smart, to take it as it comes, to think: whatever. Don't worry about whether you ever see him again.

She lies back down.

Oh. My. God.

She covers her mouth to stop speaking.

Don't. Don't. Don't say it.

Three MEN *at the end of the night.*

MEN: I get it. I do. I get that there's a way to talk, that it's in the talking, partly at least.
I get it too, that once you let it slip …
Let it slide over like down into a pit …
There's no getting out.
Once you start there's no going back.
And it can start all innocent.
A joke.
A bit of fun.
Teasing.
Where's the harm, you think.
A bit of a laugh.
Funny.
A lark.
Just us blokes.
Relaxed, getting slack, saying whatever comes.
Letting rip.
Show us your tits!
No fucking bullshit censorship.
Ugly talk.
Sure is.
Ugly.

IN THE CLUB

Ugly.
And hilarious.
Fucking funny.
Here we go, here we go.
No.
Don't do it.
Fuck, don't.
I'd …
No, don't!

   Pause.

I'd fuck her.
Oh, my god!
I'd fuck her.
I'd fuck her.
I'd fuck her too.
Nothing in it.
A bit of crap.
Nothing in it.
I'd fuck that.
I'd fuck that.
And that.
Ugly talk.
Ugly.
Like …
Stop.
Stop!
Don't go there.
Slut!
Slag!
Cunt!
Leering sneering gutter-mouthed stuff.
Cruel.
The crueller the better.
Fat bitch.
Slack mole.
Fucking dyke.

The more the better.
Skank, slut, slag, slit, piece of shit.
Once it starts …
… it's hard to resist.
It is.
It is.
To walk away from it.
It is.
To say, hey, hey, that's enough of that.
Don't say that.
Pull your fucking head in, you dickhead.
Loosen up. Lighten up. It's a joke.
A joke.
A fucking joke.
That's all.
Nothing in it.
Utter bullshit.
That's what it is.
Words.
That's right.
Words.
Get over it.
Grow a thicker skin.
Take it on the chin.

Pause.

That's enough of this.
Okay, okay.
Yeah yeah, enough.
I'm fucked.
Rooted.
Had a great night.
The best.

OLIVIA *rises from the bed.*

OLIVIA: No-one looks at me. No eye contact. None. Like I'm not there. Like I don't exist, not really, not much. I think, no way, this can't be real, this can't be happening to me. Any moment Angus will come through the door and get back into bed.

It's amazingly polite—no swearing, no-one calls me names. A few speak. You're right, you're right, someone says. You're doing great, says someone else. Not a word from me. Not a sound. Silent. Overwhelmed? I am. Overpowered? For sure. Filled with grief? Yes.

Angus. Angus, where the hell are you?

I open my eyes and see a line of men at the end of the bed.

There are guys in the room, some masturbating while others watch on. They speak amongst themselves, laughing like it's all a bit of fun.

Did you arrange this? Angus? Did you?

After two hours it ends. Alright, guys, she's had enough, someone says. They sit around for a while, on the bed, on the floor, a couple of them light up smokes. They talk a bit, very low, about what I don't know until someone asks: anyone want another go. I close my eyes and then, and only then, I whisper. No.

They leave the room. Someone's desperate for a beer, another needs a piss, others off to bed. They leave without uttering a single word to me.

On the way out, I pass someone in the passage and he tweaks my nipple. He tweaks my nipple, for god's sake.

And where's Angus? Nowhere to be found.

Months later.

In the street. OLIVIA *meets* ANGUS. *They stop still, both in shock. He goes to pass, she goes to pass. They block each other—the usual routine. They stop.*

Silence.

OLIVIA: We made love together.

 Silence.

  I thought it was great.

 Silence.

  I thought you liked me.

ANGUS: I did.
OLIVIA: How could that be?

Silence.

You say, I didn't care for you in the least. I didn't care for you at all.
ANGUS: That's not true.
OLIVIA: And you say, that's just how it is.
ANGUS: Olivia …
OLIVIA: You leant down and kissed me. I won't be long you said, and then you left me.
ANGUS: I didn't know.
OLIVIA: You knew.
ANGUS: I thought you'd tell them to go.
OLIVIA: No, you didn't think that.
ANGUS: I thought if you didn't want them to …
OLIVIA: No, you didn't think that.
ANGUS: I was told you …
OLIVIA: And you believed that was true?
ANGUS: There wasn't anything I could do.

She goes to pass and he blocks her.

Lots of girls, you should see them, they're happy to go along. In the end it was up to you.

She goes to pass.

ANGUS *grows emotional.*

Wait. I want you to know, I didn't want that to happen to you, I didn't mean for it to go that way. Once it started, I didn't know how to stop it, didn't know how to make it go away. It got out of hand, out of control, and I knew there was nothing I could do.
OLIVIA: Are you crying? Are you? Don't you dare. Don't shed a tear. Do you hear? Not a single drop.

Silence.

You say, you were nothing to me.

Silence.

You say, you were nothing to me. Nothing at all.

They walk away.

ANNIE *stands in light.*

She wears a footy jumper and shorts.

ANNIE: What's this? Oh my god, am I imagining it? Is this some feeling I've got? In my feet? In my hands? Is this blood I feel pumping through my veins? Is this my heartbeat? Is it my breath I hear, my chest rising and my brow that's beaded in sweat?

I still hear the whispers behind my back. I catch them pointing: that's her, the crazy one. She's the bitch who wanted to destroy some young footballer's life, who really only wanted to be in the limelight. I still call sometimes, turn up and cause a ruckus, make a fuss. Let them know I don't give up.

I've joined a team, a footy team, rough as guts, tough, fearless they call us. We are. Wild as can be. I'm recognising more and more of me. Bit by bit. A bit of the old grace, a bit of the speed, the old agility, good hands and something else. Something I never had. The ability to stick, to stay in, to keep a grip. Not let go. Like a wild, clawing thing.

THE END

Melita Jurisic as Bernadette in the Melbourne Theatre Company's 2018 production of THE HOUSE OF BERNARDA ALBA. (Photo: Jeff Busby)

THE HOUSE OF BERNADETTE

An adaptation of Federico Garcia Lorca's
The House of Bernarda Alba

The House of Bernadette was first produced as *The House of Bernarda Alba* by Melbourne Theatre Company at the Fairfax Studio, Arts Centre, Melbourne, on 25 May 2018 with the following cast:

MARTI	Candy Bowers
ANGELA	Peta Brady
PENELOPE	Julie Forsyth
MAGDA	Bessie Holland
MARIA	Sue Jones
BERNADETTE	Melita Jurisic
ADELE	Emily Milledge

Director, Leticia Cáceres
Assistant Director, Cassandra Fumi
Set and Costume Designer, Marg Horwell
Lighting Designer, Rachel Burke
Composer, Irine Vela
Sound Designer, Jethro Woodward

CHARACTERS

BERNADETTE, age 60
MARIA, Bernadette's mother, age 80
ANGELA, Bernadette's daughter, age 39
MARTI, Bernadette's daughter, age 25
MAGDA, Bernadette's daughter, age 30
ADELE, Bernadette's daughter, age 16
PENELOPE, Bernadette's old friend, age 60

ACT ONE

SCENE ONE

It's hot. Very hot. A great brooding silence fills a large white-tiled room stained by red dust.

An enormous fan moves laboriously overhead.

Outside, bells begin to toll.

Five women, BERNADETTE *and her four daughters*—ANGELA, MARTI, MAGDA *and* ADELE—*dressed in funereal black, appear in a line-up of cell-like rooms.*

One weeps piteously. MARTI.

They disappear.

PENELOPE *enters. She makes a beeline to a table laden with food. She stands at the table and at regular intervals stuffs sausages greedily into her mouth.*

PENELOPE: Two hours of unbelievable bullshit! About the virtues of Tony Alba! You've got to be kidding! Virtues? Tony? None. It got interesting when Marti fainted. The only one who loved her father, which isn't surprising because he was such a shit. I'm starving! I could think of nothing except these sausages and that's not what you should be thinking about at a funeral, even if it is Tony's funeral, and I knew later Bernadette would be watching me like a hawk. What you going to do now, Bernadette? Stuck with four girls. Four ugly girls. Four of them. Who'd want that? Especially Angela who's old and got no tits. But here's a twist, Angela might be coming into some money at least. A lot of it. A great big fat trust fund and all for Angela. Angela. Rich. That's a switch.

She checks the door before shoving another sausage into her gob.

How I'd love to tell Bernadette what a tight-arse, mean-minded bitch she is. I've been your friend for forty years, Bernadette, and worked my guts out helping you with the house. Forty years washing your sheets, forty years eating your leftovers, forty years of looking after you and the kids, and you're that tight. She constantly reminds me that I'm here at her mercy, that I'm lucky she and Tony took me in and if they hadn't I'd probably be on the street. Yes it's true, I had nowhere else to go, but I didn't expect to be treated like your servant, Bernadette, and I didn't expect to put up with Tony feeling me up every chance he could get!

MARIA: [*within*] Bernadette!

PENELOPE: Shit! I hope you're still locked up.

MARIA: [*within*] Bernadette!

PENELOPE: [*shouting*] She's coming!

She shoves another sausage in her mouth.

She's coming alright, with that cold little smile of hers, to see if everything is clean enough. Dust, she says. Dust, dust, dust. The dust sneaks in under doors and between cracks, coating our clothes and our bedsheets. It salts the plates off which we eat. The house would be buried in it within a week. It exhausts me. And what can I do about it? Nothing. I'm used to nothing. I was born with nothing and I'll die with nothing. And for now I'll bark when I'm told to, but I dream of the day when I'll turn and bite the hand that feeds me, and tell her, fuck you.

She bites hard into a sausage.

I've got to admit that bloody priest was a bit sweet. When he sang and his voice went up like a pitcher filling with water, it was glorious. And when he sang 'Amen', it was as if a wolf had snuck into the church.

Imitating him:

A-a-a-a-men!

She coughs.

Oh my god, I've strained my voice.

She makes a lewd gesture with her hips.

I'd rather have strained something else.

She laughs and puts the rest of the sausage into her mouth.

BERNADETTE *enters, followed by her four daughters*—ANGELA, MARTI, MAGDA *and* ADELE.

BERNADETTE: Silence!

As if at her command, the bells stop.

Thank Christ!

PENELOPE, *her mouth full, faces the table and hurriedly chews.*

Penelope?

PENELOPE *attempts to cover by feigning tears.*

What are you up to?
PENELOPE: I'm upset, of course.
BERNADETTE: Bullshit!

MARTI *sobs.*

Marti! Will you stop that?! And if you can't, go cry in your room.
MAGDA: Mum! Can't you let them be sad?
BERNADETTE: Penelope's not sad. Penelope doesn't feel sadness.
MAGDA: She feels sad like anybody else feels sad.

BERNADETTE *picks up the platter of sausages.*

BERNADETTE: Half a dozen sausages have helped comfort Penelope in her sorrow.

She hands the platter to PENELOPE.

And take out some beers. They're drinking on the patio.

As PENELOPE *leaves:*

Don't go more than a few rounds otherwise they'll be here until they're pissed off their heads.

PENELOPE *exits.*

Thank god that's over. Who was there? Every Tom, Dick and Harry. All the locals.
MAGDA: Dad used to drink with them at the pub.
MARTI: There were so many.
BERNADETTE: How many freeloaders, that's what I'd like to know?
MARTI: If they didn't know him, they knew of him. He was someone they would've heard about.
BERNADETTE: He was indeed.
ANGELA: Lots of his old business associates were there.
BERNADETTE: Looking to be paid back the money he owed, I bet.

ADELE: Lots of women I didn't recognise.

BERNADETTE: Yes, yes, let's not go there. Who brought that little girl? She was chattering through the entire bloody service.

ANGELA: She's one of the miner's daughters.

BERNADETTE: Little girls, especially chatty little girls, should not be allowed at funerals. I hope I never have to see any of them again. Don't let them come to my funeral, please! I'd wake from the dead and scream if they did. And while I had the chance, I'd give that little girl a good smack!

MARTI: I think it's nice they came.

BERNADETTE: A bunch of back-biting arseholes looking down their noses.

MAGDA: Some of them have come from miles.

BERNADETTE: They come in droves, at almighty speeds in their enormous four-wheel drives. Across the desert plains. Nothing else to come to, nothing else apart from the occasional death to draw them out. They love a death around here. A chance to step out and show off their fine clothes, a chance to snoop inside someone else's house, to gossip about the state of their affairs.

MARTI: It's Dad's funeral!

BERNADETTE: Sniffing about like we're some kind of lame duck, circling like drooling wolves, in for the kill, to take over, to buy cheap, to clean up while we're down on our luck.

MAGDA: What the fuck! They've come to Dad's funeral!

BERNADETTE: Magda, language please!

MARTI: They've come to pay their respects!

BERNADETTE: Of course they have, darling.

MARTI: He was a good man.

BERNADETTE: Of course he was, sweet.

MARTI: He was the best.

BERNADETTE: Yes, yes, Marti, why don't you go to your room and have a really good weep?

MARTI: Dad had so many friends.

BERNADETTE: Friends! Is that what you call them? Old men, from his numerous clubs, from the racecourse, from around the poker tables.

MARTI: And young friends.

PENELOPE enters and picks up another platter.

PENELOPE: Peter Romano was there.

The responses to this name come fast.

ADELE: I saw him.
MARTI: I saw him.
ANGELA: I saw him too.
MAGDA: Peter Romano's as thick as a brick.
ANGELA, ADELE and MARTI: [*together*] He is not!
BERNADETTE: Lovely that is, it's your father's funeral and there you are ogling Peter Romano.
ANGELA: Not ogling. Just looking. Just looking, that's all.

BERNADETTE *takes in* ANGELA*'s interest in Peter Romano.*

BERNADETTE: Angela? I'm surprised.
ANGELA: I said, I was just looking. He was there, and I looked at him. It was an accident really.

ADELE *scoffs*.

BERNADETTE: You would think that on this day of all days the only man you'd be looking at would be the priest.
PENELOPE: I couldn't take my eyes off him. He was a bit of alright, wasn't he?
BERNADETTE: Oh, please!

PENELOPE *exits with the platter.*

MARTI *begins to cry again.*

Marti, that's enough!
MARTI: I miss him, that's all.
BERNADETTE: Yes, yes, well you'll have plenty of time to grieve, right here, in this house. For the next eight weeks.
DAUGHTERS: [*together*] Eight weeks.

It truly dawns on them.

Eight weeks!
MARTI: No way!
MAGDA: I can't!
ADELE: What about school?
BERNADETTE: I've told the school you won't be back. What's the point? Your grades are poor and the fees are over the top.

ADELE: Fine by me.

MAGDA: I can't.

BERNADETTE: I know you dropped out of university over a year ago, Magda. I've given notice to your *flatmate*.

MAGDA: You what?

BERNADETTE: You heard me.

MAGDA: You can't do that!

BERNADETTE: And, Marti, you might as well be here because you haven't been turning up at your job and your father's no longer here to send you money to prop you up.

MARTI: I've been depressed.

BERNADETTE: Now you can be depressed at home.

ADELE: What about Ange?

BERNADETTE: Angela has been here all year. She came home for a rest.

ADELE: A rest?

ANGELA: Yes, I wasn't feeling well.

BERNADETTE: She's been looked after by her mother.

MARTI: She's been home all year?

ANGELA: Didn't you hear what Mum said? I needed a rest.

BERNADETTE: Eight weeks.

DAUGHTERS: [*together*] Eight weeks!

BERNADETTE: That's all I'm asking. Eight weeks …

DAUGHTERS: [*together*] Eight weeks.

BERNADETTE: … here, to mourn your father, to show your respects, to be together, to be with me.

The DAUGHTERS *look at their mother in appalled silence.*

Good. That's settled then. Oh yes, and when I say here, I mean here, at the house.

DAUGHTERS: [*together*] What?!

BERNADETTE: No trips into town. No shopping. No gallivanting about. Your father has died, remember. You will behave impeccably. You will grieve in a manner that is expected of you.

    MARTI *snivels.*

Yes, Marti, you are a great example to us! For eight weeks we will appear and behave with dignity and decency. We will present the perfect picture of grief.

Together the DAUGHTERS *take out their mobiles to make calls. Their phones are dead.*

I've suspended the phone service.

The DAUGHTERS *collectively express their grief.*

Your excess fees are way out of hand. Don't worry, you can still ring triple 0. Mind you, it will take them a day or two to get to you. You can still endlessly play Candy …

ANGELA: Crush.

BERNADETTE: … which is what Angela has spent hour upon hour on these last months. You can peruse your photographs. And set your alarms to rouse you from your afternoon naps. Oh …

She pulls the modem from the wall.

… and no internet.

The DAUGHTERS *collectively express their anger.*

DAUGHTERS: [*together*] No!

BERNADETTE: No on-line shopping. Whatever you want, too bad, you have plenty.

And collectively, they sulk.

MARIA: [*within*] Bernadette! Let me out!

PENELOPE *enters in a hurry.*

PENELOPE: Your mother's going berserk.

BERNADETTE: Let her out.

PENELOPE *exits.*

Eight weeks gives me time to deal with the business of your father's death and to deliberate on our future.

MARIA: [*within*] She gives me dishwater to drink. And dog meat to …

PENELOPE *enters with* MARIA *who is decked out in jewellery and a dress that's very girly.* PENELOPE *holds a cloth to* MARIA*'s mouth.*

PENELOPE: I had to stuff a tea towel in her mouth to gag her. Did you hear her?!

BERNADETTE: Take her out the back.

MARIA *bites* PENELOPE*'s hand and escapes her. The gag drops. Excited, she takes a pose.*

MARIA: I'm off to be married.

The DAUGHTERS *laugh.*

I'm to be wed, I tell you. I am. I am. How do I look?
BERNADETTE: Like a mad old chook.
MARTI: You look beautiful, Grandma.
MARIA: [*to* MARTI] More beautiful than you.

Feeling the comment undeserving, MARTI *sobs.*

MARIA *shares the insult with the other* DAUGHTERS.

Or you. Or you. Or you. No-one in their right mind would marry any one of you.
ADELE: Bitch.
ANGELA: Bitch.
MAGDA: Such a bitch.
MARIA: And you're—

PENELOPE *stuffs the gag back in* MARIA*'s mouth.*

BERNADETTE: Make sure she doesn't take off.
PENELOPE: Don't worry, I won't lose her.
BERNADETTE: I wouldn't mind if you did. Make sure the guests don't see her.
ANGELA: Why not? There might be someone out there who'd like to marry her.
MAGDA: Hey, Grandma, Peter Romano's a good catch!

PENELOPE *takes* MARIA *off.*

The guests on the patio are becoming rowdy.

BERNADETTE *faces the door to the patio.*

BERNADETTE: The quicker we get this over and done with the better.

She takes a step and stops. She addresses her DAUGHTERS.

It's a wake, remember?

The DAUGHTERS *nod.*

Not a party.

They nod.

Behave yourselves.

They nod.

I'll be watching you.

BERNADETTE *lifts her finger in warning. She takes a big breath and exits.*

Her DAUGHTERS *take a platter of food from the table and in procession follow her out.*

SCENE TWO

Silence. The wake is over.

PENELOPE *enters carrying a tray laden with empty beer bottles. She exits and the distinct sound of bottle on bottle is heard as she empties them into a recycle bin.*

The DAUGHTERS *enter, excitedly chattering.*

MAGDA: Oh my god!
ANGELA: Unbelievable.
MARTI: Outrageous.
ADELE: What?
ANGELA: Unbelievable.
MARTI: Shocking.
MAGDA: Oh my god!
ADELE: What? What?
ANGELA: She should be stopped.
MARTI: She should be shot.
MAGDA: She's out of control, that's what.
ADELE: What did she do?

PENELOPE *returns with the now empty tray.*

PENELOPE: Who?
MAGDA: Rosie's been at it again.
ADELE: At what?!
PENELOPE: Rosie? What's this about Rosie?
ANGELA: They were talking about her latest antics.
MAGDA: In way too much detail.
PENELOPE: Leave Rosie alone.

PENELOPE *exits.*

ADELE: Tell me. Tell me.
ANGELA: You're too young, Adele.
ADELE: I know more about life than you, Angela.
MAGDA: We shouldn't be talking about this stuff at all.

They feign propriety.

MARTI: No, it's not right.
MAGDA: It's not.
ANGELA: It's terrible, in fact.
MAGDA: Poor Rosie.
MARTI: Poor Rosie.
ANGELA: Poor, poor Rosie.

A long pause. They resume gossiping.

MARTI: She was screaming her head off.
ADELE: Oh my god!
MARTI: 'Come on, come on, bring it on!'
ANGELA: Cursing from the top of her lungs.
ADELE: Oh my god!
ANGELA: 'I'll fucking take you all on!'
MAGDA: They propped her up in the back of the ute.
ADELE: Really?!
MAGDA: And drove off …
MARTI: … into the desert …
ANGELA: … her dress all undone …
ADELE: No!
MAGDA: … her tits hanging out …
ADELE: No!
MARTI: … on show for everyone.
ANGELA: She's shameless.

PENELOPE *enters with tray laden.*

PENELOPE: It's them who are shameless.
MAGDA: They picked up some other blokes on the way.
ANGELA: She takes them all on, they say.
ADELE: Oh my god! Really?
PENELOPE: The bastards won't let Rosie alone.

And PENELOPE *exits. The sound of bottles in the recycle bin.*

MARTI: She loves it.
ADELE: Does she?
ANGELA: Of course she does.

> PENELOPE *reappears.*

PENELOPE: I doubt it.
MARTI: She does.
PENELOPE: I don't think so.
ANGELA: She does.
MAGDA: She laughs her head off.

> ADELE *laughs her head off.*

PENELOPE: They're after and after her like a pack of dogs.
MARTI: It's not our local boys.
MAGDA: They were done with Rosie years ago.
ANGELA: It's the miners, we know.
MAGDA: Taking it in turns to have a go.
ADELE: Oh my god!
PENELOPE: Dogs. Dogs is what they are.

> PENELOPE *exits.*

ANGELA: She's not from here.
MARTI: She's from way, way out.
MAGDA: From some remote community.
MARTI: What's the name of her mob?
ANGELA: Too hard to pronounce.
MARTI: Boys love a black girl.
ANGELA: They get so excited.
MARTI: They suck their fingers.
ANGELA: They lick their lips.
MAGDA: They pull their …

> ADELE *shrieks with excitement.*

> PENELOPE *enters with more bottles.*

PENELOPE: Stop this!

> BERNADETTE *enters.*

BERNADETTE: Stop what? What are you talking about?

> *Silence.*

PENELOPE: It's Rosie. The usual stuff.
BERNADETTE: [*slightly alarmed*] Rosie? Why? What's going on?
MAGDA: They took her way out bush.
MARTI: And brought her back sitting up in the back of the ute.
MAGDA: With no clothes on.
ADELE: With no clothes on!
ANGELA: Not a stitch.
MAGDA: Her hair all wild.
MARTI: A crown of tumbleweed on her head.
BERNADETTE: This kind of talk makes me sick.
MAGDA: It's not as if we haven't heard it all before.
BERNADETTE: I don't want to hear talk like this.

Abashed, the DAUGHTERS *drop their heads.*

I don't want you to listen to these stories from these bloody horrible men.

Their heads drop lower still.

Or repeat them. You should be above all this. Rosie, Rosie, Rosie.

Silence.

I don't want to hear about Rosie again.

Pause.

And must I remind you: we buried your father today?

They bite their lips. MARTI *immediately sobs.*

All of you, go. Now. Go to your rooms.

The DAUGHTERS *exit.*

They appear for a moment in their cell-like rooms, on display with their arms crossed, or on their hips, belligerent.

Is that the way for them to talk?

PENELOPE *shrugs.*

Is that the kind of conversation they should be engaged in?

She shrugs.

I don't think so. I don't want them talking or listening to this kind of stuff about Rosie. Most of her mob took off years ago. Why's she still here?

PENELOPE: Bernadette, you know why she's still here.

BERNADETTE *is struck by* PENELOPE's *statement, but quickly moves on.*

BERNADETTE: I want them to be decent. That kind of talk is coarse and wild.

PENELOPE: Hardly.

BERNADETTE: I expected more from them. Signs of their good breeding; more cultured, better spoken, smarter, at least one of them to have a little business acumen. Those bloody private schools and their snotty-nosed bullshit. The very best, top dollar no less, and what do I get? Useless, the lot of them.

PENELOPE: I can understand your disappointment—not much chop, any one of them.

BERNADETTE: They need to be tethered, to be corralled in.

PENELOPE: Get them husbands. No worries about them going wild then.

BERNADETTE: There's plenty of time for marriage.

PENELOPE: Girls get a bit feisty without men.

BERNADETTE: Oh, for god's sake, Penelope! None of them have boyfriends. So what?!

PENELOPE: All I'm saying is if you want to settle them.

BERNADETTE: With anyone?

PENELOPE: No. With someone they like.

BERNADETTE: [*slight pretentiousness*] There's no-one within thousands of kilometres good enough.

PENELOPE: They might fall in love, you know.

BERNADETTE: You think love is what's most important for a successful marriage.

PENELOPE: I think it's not bad, a bit of love, why not?

BERNADETTE: Marriage didn't do much for you. Especially when he pissed off and left you with nothing.

PENELOPE: That's true, I suppose, but I'm glad …

BERNADETTE: That you had love? Love gave you nothing. Lots of tears, and the clothes on your back.

PENELOPE: There needs to be a bit of love, surely, a little bit.

BERNADETTE: I've just buried a man I thought I loved. I thought he was handsome. Thought he was smart, charming, going to give me a good life. I thought I needed him. What I needed was an optometrist, I needed my head read, I needed someone to tell me not to marry him and make a run for it instead.

PENELOPE: He did turn out somewhat of a disappointment, the old Tony.

BERNADETTE: A greedy, greedy man with a penchant for unborn veal and Grange wines which he poured in enormous quantities down his extremely fat neck. What an appetite he had! The planes, the boats, the holidays abroad. How he'd spoil the girls: anything you want, here it's yours. How he spent, spent, spent. The incessant gambling. This man I thought I loved, the great pig of a man could have blown it all.

PENELOPE: I know you, you'll get it back,

BERNADETTE: I'll take care of the matter of my daughters' marriages from the experience of a woman who knows marriage and has had two, the first a very lucrative arrangement and the second a bloody financial disaster.

PENELOPE: Some of your girls are getting on.

BERNADETTE: I'm not letting my daughters be seduced by useless men with no prospects. They will not fall prey to shysters. They're easy pickings, my daughters are.

PENELOPE: Can't say I've noticed a long queue.

BERNADETTE: Marti fell for a man who glanced in her direction she was so hungry for affection. Magda needs a strong man, someone who can manage the contempt she feels for men. Adele is young and flighty. I don't need to do anything about Adele for quite some time. And Angela ...

PENELOPE: Angela is no spring chicken. How old is she now?

BERNADETTE: Exactly thirty-nine.

PENELOPE: God! And she's never had a man.

BERNADETTE: Angela has no interest.

PENELOPE: She does appear to have no juice in her.

BERNADETTE: No, not much.

PENELOPE: But I have noticed of late, signs of life.

BERNADETTE: Angela?

PENELOPE: A bit of a yearning perhaps.

BERNADETTE: Angela? I don't think so.

PENELOPE: Lots of telltale sighs. And once the word is out ...

BERNADETTE *waves to quieten* PENELOPE.

BERNADETTE: She'll have a dozen hungry dingoes tracking her.
PENELOPE: I imagine there'll be quite a few knocking on her door once they've heard. They'll be trying to kick the door in.
BERNADETTE: They can knock and kick all they like.

A loud knocking.

MAGDA *enters.*

MAGDA: Mum, there's a man at the door. A lawyer. He wants to talk to you. [*Surprised*] And Angela.

BERNADETTE *pulls herself together.*

BERNADETTE: Call Angela.

They exit.

SCENE THREE

MARTI *stands in the centre of the room. Forlornly, she cries.*

MAGDA *enters and watches her for a while.*

MAGDA: Come on, Marti.
MARTI: I'm alright.
MAGDA: Don't cry.
MARTI: It's okay.
MAGDA: Have you been taking your pills?
MARTI: Yeah.
MAGDA: Do they do any good?
MARTI: No.
MAGDA: Sometimes they take a while to kick in.
MARTI: I've been taking them for years.
MAGDA: Don't be sad.
MARTI: I've always been sad.
MAGDA: Can't you stop?
MARTI: I don't think I can.
MAGDA: Stop, Marti, stop.
MARTI: I want Victoria.
MAGDA: She'd make you laugh.
MARTI: She would.

MAGDA: She wasn't at the funeral.
MARTI: You can guess why.
MAGDA: Of course, I can.
MARTI: Gary won't let her out the front door.
MAGDA: Such a fucking shithead!
MARTI: He won't let her go out.
MAGDA: Won't let her see her friends.
MARTI: Me. He won't let her see me.
MAGDA: Wants to know where she is every moment of the day.
MARTI: Won't let her wear what she wants.
MAGDA: No make-up.
MARTI: None.
MAGDA: Not allowed to use the phone.
MARTI: Not allowed to go out alone.
MAGDA: Penelope saw her at the supermarket covered in bruises.
MARTI: The last time I saw her she was looking over her shoulder the entire time.
MAGDA: Why would anyone want a fucking boyfriend, that's what I want to know?
MARTI: Because it's expected, I suppose.
MAGDA: She won't leave him.
MARTI: I know.
MAGDA: It's all she knows. Remember Victoria's father.
MARTI: And the grandfather.
MAGDA: Another wife-bashing arsehole.
MARTI: It's in their genes.
MAGDA: And the women take it.
MARTI: They do.
MAGDA: She'll never get away.
MARTI: She'll never get away.
MAGDA: Never, I'm sad to say.
MARTI: He should be in jail.
MAGDA: For bashing your girlfriend? Forget it.
MARTI: Poor Victoria.
MAGDA: I'd love to be part of a vigilante group and go around and smash in his head.
MARTI: That'd be good.

MAGDA: Could wait in the bushes for him with a baseball bat.
MARTI: That'd work.
MAGDA: Run him down in a car.
MARTI: Even better.
MAGDA: Better not to have anything to do with men.
MARTI: I'd like one.
MAGDA: What?
MARTI: A man. I'd like one.
MAGDA: Really?
MARTI: Yes, I would. I really would.
MAGDA: Always got to be the best, always the smartest, the toughest, the fucking loudest. They're sleazy, men are. One lecturer I had was always on the prowl, licking his lips, sniffing around for the next pretty young thing.

She shudders.

When I was a kid I was afraid to grow up because one of them might take me in his arms.

MARTI: I thought I'd grow up and someone would take me in his arms, and I'd be happy.

She sobs.

MAGDA: James wanted you.

It's as if MAGDA *has struck* MARTI.

MARTI: James. I waited for him once in a hotel room. I'd bought a slinky nightgown, maroon it was with a cream lace edge. I waited all night long but he never came. He'd rung me. He'd made all the arrangements. He'd booked the room. There was even champagne, but he never came. And I never heard from him again. I heard he married someone else.

MAGDA: I always thought that James loved you.

MARTI: [*in tears*] I know, I know, I thought so too. I'd been so sure he'd come. Never for a moment did I doubt it.

ANGELA, *all smug smiles, enters. She's sprightly on her feet.*

ANGELA: What are you two doing?
MARTI: Nothing.
ANGELA: That'd be right. Can't you find something to do?

MAGDA: Like what?
ANGELA: Something useful.
MARTI: Like what?
ANGELA: Something to earn your keep.
MARTI: What?!
MAGDA: Angela, fuck off.

Humming, ANGELA *exits.*

They stare after her.

I think that was Angela happy.

They exit.

SCENE FOUR

BERNADETTE *enters with* PENELOPE *close on her heels.*

PENELOPE: That's a lot of money in trust for Angela.
BERNADETTE: Yes.
PENELOPE: An incredible amount.
BERNADETTE: Yes.
PENELOPE: So much.
BERNADETTE: Yes.
PENELOPE: And for the others considerably less.
BERNADETTE: Yes. Yes. Yes. You've said so three times now, when you know I don't want to hear it. Considerably less; a lot less. Nothing in fact. Don't go on and on about it.
PENELOPE: And for you …
BERNADETTE: Didn't you hear what I just said?
PENELOPE: … nothing. Nothing at all.
BERNADETTE: Yes, Penelope, that's right!
PENELOPE: That's it? What happened to the cash?
BERNADETTE: All gone. All of it. Tony pissed it up against the wall. In fact, there are a great number of debts.
PENELOPE: Shit, Bernadette! What are you going to do?
BERNADETTE: I'm going to tell you to go away, now. Go, clean the house, go, before I wring the life out of you.

PENELOPE *exits.*

BERNADETTE *lets herself go for a moment. She lifts her head and cries in anguish.*

Shit! Shit, shit, shit.

ANGELA *enters and immediately* BERNADETTE *pulls herself together.*

ANGELA *wears an ill-fitting frock. Her face is made up, her hair is piled up on her head and she wears high heels which make it difficult for her to walk with grace, but there's a confidence about her nonetheless.*

Angela!

ANGELA: Mother.

BERNADETTE: Oh, Angela, don't be ridiculous. What do you think you're doing on the day your father's been put to rest?

ANGELA: He wasn't my father. Mine died a long time ago. You seem to have forgotten that?

BERNADETTE: You owe more to this man, the father of your sisters, than to your own.

ANGELA: I'm not so sure about that.

BERNADETTE: Thanks to him, your fortune is intact.

ANGELA: How come I didn't know that I had a fortune?

BERNADETTE: Your father was smart enough to look after it for you.

ANGELA: He wasn't my father.

BERNADETTE: Your stepfather looked after it for you.

ANGELA: For me? I don't think so. Otherwise I might have been told about it. But no, I've been left in the dark.

BERNADETTE: He did well by you.

ANGELA: How come I wasn't told that everyone has been living off a trust I didn't know a thing about?

BERNADETTE: You were a child.

ANGELA: It should have been paid to me when I was twenty-one.

BERNADETTE: You've done fine.

ANGELA: The money was mine!

BERNADETTE: And now you have it.

ANGELA: I should've had it eighteen years ago.

BERNADETTE: Listen to you.

ANGELA: Eighteen years ago! *My* father put it in trust for *me* all those years ago.

BERNADETTE: You've had everything a young woman could ask for.
ANGELA: I could've had so much more.
BERNADETTE: Angela, what is it you think you've missed out on?
ANGELA: A life. How about that? I've missed out on a life!
BERNADETTE: A life?
ANGELA: I'm going out.
BERNADETTE: Where to?
ANGELA: I don't know. I'm going out. Just out. Out.
BERNADETTE: No, you're not.
ANGELA: I can if I want to.
BERNADETTE: No, you're not.
ANGELA: You can't stop me.
BERNADETTE: You're behaving like an ungrateful spoiled brat.
ANGELA: I'd be careful how you spoke to me if I was you.

BERNADETTE slaps ANGELA's face.

BERNADETTE: I decide what you do.

They exit in opposite directions.

SCENE FIVE

The DAUGHTERS stand at the entrances of their rooms. ANGELA has an enormous smile on her face while her SISTERS, mouths agape, look appalled.

MAGDA: Nothing?
MARTI: Nothing?
ADELE: Nothing?
MAGDA, MARTI and ADELE: [*together*] Nothing at all?
ANGELA: That's right.
MAGDA: You get the lot?
ANGELA: I do.
MAGDA: Fuck off!
ADELE: I don't believe it.
MARTI: I don't believe it.
MAGDA: Nor do I.
MARTI: Dad would leave us something.
ANGELA: He had nothing to leave.
ADELE: Dad had plenty of money.

ANGELA: It wasn't his.
MARTI: He would've left something to me.
ANGELA: Not a brass razoo.

The SISTERS *follow* ANGELA *into the room.*

MAGDA: What about the land? And the livestock? What about his latest investment: the stud cattle?
ANGELA: Not his.
MAGDA: He had shares. Millions of them.
ANGELA: Not. His.
MARTI: The house?
MAGDA: Not the house?
ADELE: No way!

ANGELA *nods.*

MAGDA: Fuck off!
MARTI: Mum?

ANGELA *shakes her head.*

ADELE: Not a thing?
MAGDA: Fuck off!
ADELE: That's not right.
MARTI: It's not fair.
ANGELA: It is what it is, and what it is, is that it all belongs to me.
MAGDA: All of it?
ANGELA: Yes.
MARTI: All yours?
ANGELA: Ah-huh. Mine. All mine.

Pause.

ADELE: Keep it, I don't care.
ANGELA: You might.
MAGDA: Shut up, Adele.
ADELE: We don't want it, so relax.
ANGELA: You say that now.
MARTI: Shut up, Adele.
ADELE: It's all yours.
ANGELA: I'm well aware of that.
MARTI and MAGDA: [*together*] Adele, shut up!

ADELE: As far as I'm concerned you can hang on to it all.
ANGELA: I just might do that.

> PENELOPE *enters.*

PENELOPE: Guess who just pulled up out front?
MAGDA: Who?
PENELOPE: Peter Romano, that's who.

> ADELE *steps forward eagerly.*

He's come to see Angela.

> *Pause.*

MAGDA, MARTI and ADELE: [*together*] What?!

> PENELOPE *is as surprised as anyone.*

PENELOPE: I know!
ANGELA: What's he want?
PENELOPE: Go and find out.
ANGELA: You've made a mistake.
PENELOPE: I already asked him twice.
ANGELA: It's a joke.
PENELOPE: I promise you it's not.
ANGELA: I'm not going. I'm not.
PENELOPE: He's asked for you.
ANGELA: What about Mother?
PENELOPE: She's with him.
ANGELA: She'll deal with him. He'll soon disappear.
PENELOPE: She's poured him a beer.
ANGELA: You're sure it was for me he asked?
PENELOPE: Quick! You can't keep your gentleman caller waiting all day.

> ANGELA *stands as if frozen for a moment and then begins to giggle nervously. She looks around at her* SISTERS *who stare sullenly back. She excitedly exits.*

He's on the patio. You'd have a good view from your rooms.

> MAGDA *and* MARTI *run to their rooms where they open the shutters on their windows and lean out.*

> ADELE *stays behind.*

Aren't you going?

ADELE: Why should I? It's nothing to me.
PENELOPE: I'm not missing this for the life of me.

> PENELOPE *rushes off.*
>
> ADELE *is resolute for a moment and then quickly rushes to her room.*

SCENE SIX

MARTI and MAGDA enter fast and in shock.
They stand bewildered in the centre of the room.

MARTI: Two weeks!
MAGDA: Two weeks!
MARTI and MAGDA: [*together*] Two weeks!
MAGDA: It can't be.
MARTI: It's extraordinary.
MAGDA: It's been two weeks!
MARTI: Two weeks.
MAGDA: Two fucking weeks.
MARTI: I don't believe it.
MAGDA: Believe it.
MARTI: I can't.
MAGDA: It's true.
MARTI: He's going to marry her?
MAGDA: He is.
MARTI: It's bullshit!
MAGDA: It is.

> *Pause. They smile reluctantly.*

No, that's great.
MARTI: You're right, it is, it's great.
MAGDA: I'm glad.
MARTI: Me too.
MAGDA: They're in love.
MARTI: In love? Yeah, they're desperately in love.
MAGDA: I'm happy for them.
MARTI: Ecstatic.
MAGDA: I'm serious.

MARTI: I am too.

Pause. Their faces sour.

MAGDA: I'm not.
MARTI: Nor am I.
MAGDA: It's …
MARTI and MAGDA: [*together*] Bullshit!
MAGDA: Mum won't allow it.
MARTI: Of course not.
MAGDA: No way she'd let Angela marry that dick.
MARTI: No way.
MAGDA: The guy's a fuckwit.
MARTI: It's not as if he's come for her looks.
MAGDA: Because she's our sister we can say this.
MARTI: Because she's family and we love her.
MAGDA: And because it's the truth.
MARTI: The absolute truth.
MAGDA: Angela is sickly.
MARTI: Weak.
MAGDA: Unattractive.
MARTI: A dressed-up stick.
MAGDA: And he's twenty-five, for god's sake!
MARTI: And she's almost forty.
MAGDA: Twenty fucking five!
MARTI: And he's good-looking.
MAGDA: And she's not.
MARTI: They're a ridiculous match.
MAGDA: An enamel cup on a china plate.
MARTI: A meercat and a …
MAGDA: … hyena. How about that?
MARTI: And there are others far more likely in this very house.

ADELE *enters dressed in a tiny dress and very high heels.*

ADELE: Do you know where Mum's keys are?
MAGDA: What the …?
MARTI: If Mum sees you …
ADELE: She'll what?
MAGDA: She'll drag you by the hair, that's what.

ADELE: Do you know where the keys are or not?
MAGDA: Where do you think you're going?
ADELE: I'm going to town.
MARTI: And you're wearing that?
ADELE: Yes, I know, I look fantastic, don't I?
MAGDA: Well, don't get too excited because nobody's going to see you in it.
ADELE: I can't believe it, she's hidden the keys.
MARTI: You could wear it to Angela's wedding with Peter Romano.
ADELE: What?
MARTI: Haven't you heard?
ADELE: It's not true. You two have got to get out. You're forgetting what's make-believe.

MARTI and MAGDA cross themselves.

It can't be.

They cross themselves again.

No!

MARTI: They're in love.
ADELE: I don't believe you.
MAGDA: That's why she's been walking around with that stupid smile on her face.
ADELE: He wouldn't.
MAGDA: He would.
MARTI: He's head over heels.
ADELE: He doesn't want Angela.
MAGDA: You've got to be kidding. Angela's a prize.
ADELE: A prize?
MAGDA: A booby prize.
ADELE: No, no, no ...

ADELE desperately looks about her for an escape.

MARTI: What are you thinking, Adele?
ADELE: About being stuck here. With you.
MAGDA: Get used to it.
ADELE: I will not get used to it! I can't be locked up. I don't want to be like you two, all shrivelled up. I can't breathe. I can't believe ... I want to go out!

MARIA *enters, the tea towel draped over her head.*

MAGDA: Oh no, how did she get out?

MARIA: I ran away because I want to marry—I want to get married to a beautiful manly man from the shore of the sea. Because here the men run from women.

MARTI: Oh, Granny, shut up!

MARIA: No, no—I won't shut up. I don't want to see these single women, longing for marriage, turning their hearts to dust. I want to go out.

BERNADETTE and PENELOPE *enter. A grinning* ANGELA *follows.*

BERNADETTE: What the hell is this?

MARIA: I want to go out.

ADELE: I want to go out.

BERNADETTE: Nobody's going anywhere.

ADELE: I've got to.

BERNADETTE: We have a deal, remember.

ADELE: Please, Mum …

BERNADETTE: No-one is to leave the house. And, Adele, as if I'd let you go out looking like that.

MARIA: Bernadette, I want a man to get married to and be happy with!

BERNADETTE: Of course you do. Lock her up!

MARIA: Let me go out, Bernadette! Let me out!

PENELOPE *seizes* MARIA.

BERNADETTE: Help her, all of you!

They grab at the old woman who runs away from them.

MARIA: I want to get away from here! Bernadette! To get married by the shore of the sea—by the shore of the sea!

END OF ACT ONE

ACT TWO

SCENE SEVEN

The heat is insufferable.

The air conditioners are at full blast.

The enormous fan overhead laboriously churns the air.

PENELOPE, *on hands and knees, attempts to clean the dust from the floor.*

BERNADETTE *and her* DAUGHTERS *swelter in their cell-like rooms.* ADELE *lies on her back with her legs splayed wide against the wall.* MARTI *and* MAGDA *fan themselves furiously, sulking.* ANGELA *has spread her arms wide and looks up at the ceiling, a picture of exaltation.*

BERNADETTE *takes stock.*

BERNADETTE: I've got you. I've got you. You're mine, you're mine, you're mine. Almost slipped through my fingers, almost lost my grip, left you squandered and cheated. Almost saw the back of me, my bags packed, my shoulders slumped, walking off defeated. Almost. Holding on for dear life now, squeezing tight the memory of how close I came to losing you. Brought here a young bride to a lonely, lonely life in a pitiful land, an unwelcoming place, a wasteland, an empty, dreadful and ancient land which had sat for millions of years, utterly useless, calling out for someone to come along and do something with it; make something of it, for someone to lift its skirt and its layers of petticoats and reveal the treasure beneath them. Lying there, waiting, for the taking. For the taking. For the taking.

The WOMEN *and the rooms disappear.*

MARTI, MAGDA and ANGELA reappear, seeking relief from the heat. They enter the large room.

There's a tall pile of magazines on a coffee table.

A very hot PENELOPE *sits fanning herself with one of the magazines. Occasionally she fans between her knees.*

MARTI *and* MAGDA *languorously pick up a magazine and sit or lie on the cool tiles.*

ANGELA is all smiles. She does an awkward little pirouette. She pulls out her mobile and browses the internet.

At various times the SISTERS *take turns to stand in front of the air conditioner. They lift their tops or dresses above their heads to get maximum relief. At times they spray water in their faces.*

MARTI: [*calling out*] Adele, aren't you coming?!

A faint but very recognisable sound of moaning comes from Adele's darkened room.

MAGDA: She'll come soon.

ADELE *is doing her best. Her moans become more urgent.*

PENELOPE: Something's wrong with that one. I find her restless, trembling, frightened—as if a lizard lies between her breasts.

ADELE *climaxes.*

MARTI: There's nothing more wrong with her than there is with all of us.

MAGDA: All of us except Angela.

ANGELA: I feel fine. I feel better than fine. I feel a million dollars!

She laughs at her joke.

Actually, I feel about 87 million dollars!

And laughs some more.

Her SISTERS *look at her with loathing.*

And anyone who doesn't like it can drop dead.

ANGELA *stands over* PENELOPE *until she gets the hint and vacates the chair.*

ANGELA *sits and continues to browse the internet and* MARTI *and* MAGDA *watch on enviously.*

MAGDA: Can I borrow your phone, Angela?

ANGELA: I'm using it.

MAGDA: I won't be long.

ANGELA: Mother says I need it because of my change in circumstances. I have so much to arrange.

MAGDA: I need it to make one call.

ANGELA: I don't think so.

MAGDA: That's all.

ANGELA: Magda, as you very well know there's been a bit of trouble and the finances have yet to be settled.

MAGDA: [*sarcastic*] You know, the nicest things about you, Angela, are your figure and your lovely personality.

ANGELA: Don't you worry about my figure. Pretty soon you won't recognise it. Listen to this …

She reads from her phone.

Daniella says, 'I've always hated having a small chest and obsess about it every day. I've decided to do something about it. I want to look in proportion.'

PENELOPE *has slowly returned to dusting but conveniently in front of the air conditioner.*

PENELOPE: You are in proportion, Angela.

ANGELA: I'd like to have a cleavage.

MAGDA: Don't do it, they cut your nipples off.

ANGELA: They do not! Do they? I'd like to look good in a bikini.

MARTI: Do it. You'd look more womanly.

ANGELA: I've already booked myself in. The day after my release from this incarceration, I'm out of this hellhole and into a double D cup.

PENELOPE: A D cup! You'd be way out of proportion.

ANGELA: And onto a beach. In Phuket maybe. Strolling along in the shallows, tanned, feeling the sand beneath my feet. Holding hands …

MARTI: You've been watching too much TV.

MAGDA: Maybe you won't get released.

ANGELA: Unlike you, I have the advantage of being able to buy my way out.

Some more loathing in silence.

MARTI: If only there was a bit of a breeze.

MAGDA: I couldn't sleep because of the heat.

MARTI: Neither could I.

MAGDA: There was a black cloud but only a few miserable drops.

PENELOPE: I got up at one in the morning and the earth seemed to be on fire. Angela, I saw you were still on the patio with Peter, looking nice and cosy.

MAGDA: [*with irony*] That late! What time did he leave?

ANGELA: Why ask if you were up and about?
PENELOPE: He left about one-thirty.
ANGELA: How do you know?
PENELOPE: I heard his car go.
MARTI: But I heard him around four.
PENELOPE: At four!
ANGELA: Must have been someone else.

> ANGELA *is swiping at her photos on her phone.*

Have a look at these, Peter loves me to take his photo.

No-one takes a look.

The others flip through magazines.

PENELOPE *shows the* DAUGHTERS *a page.*

PENELOPE: Look at her then. And look at her now.
MARTI: She looks wonderful.
PENELOPE: She's seventy-five!
MAGDA: She looks much younger.

> ANGELA *joins them.*

ANGELA: She looks good. Maybe a little constantly surprised.
PENELOPE: [*reading*] She's had ... 'a neck lift, full face lift, her lower eyes and forehead done, fat transfer to the nasolabial folds and dermabrasion to the lines on her top lip'. It took eight hours and she lost a lot of blood but she looks great, doesn't she? I'd like to have a bit of a tuck here and there.

> MAGDA *and* MARTI *zone in on* ANGELA.

MAGDA: What did Peter say to you when he first came by?
ANGELA: Nothing. What should he say? He just talked.
MAGDA: It's a bit weird that two people who never knew each other should suddenly hook up and be engaged.
ANGELA: I don't think so.
MAGDA: It is a bit weird.
MARTI: You've got to admit.
ANGELA: These things just happen. A man thinks he might be interested in a woman, he hears things, he asks around and he gets the idea that she might be interested back.

MARTI: Sure, but he has to ask.
ANGELA: Of course.
MAGDA: How did he ask you?
ANGELA: No way in particular.
MARTI: Give us the picture.
ANGELA: He said, you know I've always been attracted to you and I've been looking for a good, decent sort of woman, and that's you—that is if you're agreeable.

Silence until MAGDA *and* MARTI *burst into laughter.*

MAGDA: Oh my god, that's fucking embarrassing.
ANGELA: Well, don't ask. It is embarrassing.
MARTI: So romantic.
MAGDA: Like eighteenth-century romantic.
ANGELA: I can't tell it the way it was.
MAGDA: Did he say anything else?
ANGELA: He did all the talking.
MARTI: What about you?
ANGELA: I couldn't speak. My heart was in my mouth.
MAGDA: For god's sake, why?
ANGELA: I'm not used to being alone with men at night.
MAGDA: Really?
ANGELA: Yes, really.
MARTI: She's only thirty-nine.
MAGDA: Did he kiss you?
ANGELA: Sort of.
MARTI: Sort of?
ANGELA: Yes! He kissed me.
MAGDA: Did you kiss him back?
ANGELA: I think so. I think I did.

Pause as the WOMEN *contemplate* ANGELA.

Of course I kissed him back.
MAGDA: Have you …?
ANGELA: What?
MAGDA: Have you ever …?
ANGELA: What? Yes, of course I have. Lots of times.
MARTI: How many?

ANGELA: Lots!
MAGDA: I can tell.
MARTI: It's obvious.
ANGELA: I have!

> *They back off and quietly giggle while* ANGELA *buries her head in a magazine.*
>
> PENELOPE *has reclaimed the chair.*

PENELOPE: I was sitting out on the front veranda of my house when I first saw my husband Eddie, the short arse. It was very dark. I saw him coming along the street and as he went by he said, 'Good evening'. 'Good evening,' I said. Then he stopped and we were both silent for about half an hour.

> *A very long pause takes her back.*

The sweat poured down my body. Then Eddie called across to me in a very low voice and said, 'Come on, come over here. Come for a walk with me. Come on, let's go, let me get my hands on you.'

> *They shriek with excitement.* MARTI *looks about, frantic..*

MARTI: I thought Mum was coming!
MAGDA: What's she going to do?
MARTI: She won't like it.
MAGDA: And?
ANGELA: Yes. And?
PENELOPE: And then I got up and … went for a walk with him.
MAGDA: And?
MARTI: And?
PENELOPE: I let him get his hands on me.

> *Again they shriek with excitement.*

MARTI: Shhh! She'll hear us.
MAGDA: We're listening to a story, that's all.
MARTI: You know she doesn't like these kinds of stories.
MAGDA: I'm not afraid of her.
MARTI: I'm not afraid of her either.
MAGDA: You're pissing your pants because we're listening to a bloody story.
MARTI: I'm not afraid of her.

ANGELA: I am. I've always been afraid of her.

MAGDA: It's a story, for god's sake! Go on, tell us the rest.

PENELOPE: We got married. He raised greyhounds. But let me tell you, after you're married, a man gives up the bed for the table, then the table for the pub, and all the love goes to the greyhounds and any woman who doesn't like it can go to hell.

MAGDA: You put up with that?

PENELOPE: I handled it.

MARTI: Didn't you used to hit him?

PENELOPE: I almost poked one of his eyes out once.

MAGDA: Nice one.

PENELOPE: And then he left me for a woman who was half his age. And I killed his greyhounds. With his gun. Every one.

MAGDA: [*calling*] Adele! Come quick! You're missing out on Penelope's account of the joys of wedlock!

MARTI: I'll get her.

> MARTI *exits.*

MAGDA: What's wrong with Adele?

PENELOPE: She never sleeps.

MAGDA: Is she sick?

PENELOPE: Restless is my guess.

ANGELA: She writhes about, in envy, that's what she does.

> MARTI *and* ADELE *enter.*

MARTI: I got her up.

ADELE: My body aches.

MARTI: [*suggestively*] Didn't you sleep well last night?

ADELE: Whether I was awake or asleep, it's got nothing to do with you.

MARTI: I was concerned about you!

ADELE: Concerned? Nosy more like it. I wish I was invisible so I could pass through a room without being asked where I was going every time.

MAGDA: [*her head in a magazine*] Angela, you might have to do more than your tit job. Listen to this. It's about the growing industry in labiaectomy: "The surgical management of the vulva is becoming more popular because Brazilians have revealed vaginas with unsightly flaps'.

ANGELA: What have the Brazilians got to do with it?
MAGDA: That reminds me, I'm due for a wax. By the time I'm out of here I'll have turned into a grizzly bear. Do you get rid of your hair down there?
MARTI: I've done it once but then I thought, why bother, who's going to see me, and besides I got all these lumps.
MAGDA: Do you, Adele?
ADELE: What's it to you?!
ANGELA: I don't.
MAGDA: Nobody has hair down there.
ANGELA: But I will. As soon as I can I'll get it done.
PENELOPE: You don't have to, Angela. I've still got a lovely bush.

The DAUGHTERS *are repulsed.*

DAUGHTERS: [*together*] Please!

Outside, the sound of a truck pulling up and its beeping horn draws PENELOPE *to the door.*

PENELOPE: Angela, your packages have come.

ANGELA *and* MAGDA *rush out excitedly.*

MARTI *looks fixedly at* ADELE.

ADELE: What are you looking at? What? What do you want? Can you keep your eyes to yourself for once?

MARTI *exits.*

PENELOPE: Adele, she's your sister, and actually the most loving one of the bunch.
ADELE: She follows me everywhere. Sometimes she looks in my room to see if I'm sleeping. She won't let me breathe, and she's always going, 'Oh, too bad about that face!' or 'Too bad about that body, it's going to waste'. What's she trying to do to me? I have no intention of letting this [*pointing to her face*] or this [*indicating her body*] go to waste.

SCENE EIGHT

MARTI *enters. She's furtive, looking about, up to something and taken by surprise when* MAGDA *enters.*

MAGDA: How many packages, for god's sake? The crap she's bought. Perfume? Angela? Lingerie? Dream on, Angela! How many handbags does she need? Sunglasses, about fifteen pairs. And shoes. All those shoes. The money, the money, the money she's got. She can spend it all. Until there's not one cent left. What about us? What are we going to do? It's not right. Some of that money belongs to us. Nothing, nothing, nothing for us. It's fucked, I tell you, it's fucked.

MARTI *returns to her own preoccupation.*

MARTI: I couldn't sleep a wink last night. I thought I heard someone in the garden. Late. Very late. I've heard it other nights. Could be a dingo, I suppose. Or a donkey. A young unbroken donkey. That's it! A wild little donkey.

MAGDA *starts to go.*

Magda!

MAGDA: [*at the door*] What?

Pause.

MARTI: Nothing.

Pause.

Magda!

MAGDA: What, Marti, what?

MARTI: It's alright.

MAGDA: Why did you call me?

MARTI: It just came out. I didn't mean to.

MAGDA *turns to leave.*

Do you ever feel, you know, like your body is, you know, is about to burst?

MAGDA: Shit, Marti.

MARTI: You think if only someone, someone would come along and put his hand out and touch …

MAGDA: Oh god, Marti, go lie down for a while.

MARTI: Look at us, Magda. We're gorgeous. I think we are. We are.

MAGDA: Yes, Marti, but—

MARTI: Don't we deserve to be eaten up?

MAGDA: But Marti—

MARTI: Don't we deserve to be taken in someone's arms?
MAGDA: Yes, Marti, but—
MARTI: To be cupped in the crook of their bodies?
MAGDA: Marti—
MARTI: To be touched. [*In a whisper*] I'm still waiting for James to turn up.
MAGDA: Marti, I have someone who thinks I'm gorgeous, and delicious, and wants to eat me up.
MARTI: You do?
MAGDA: I do.
MARTI: Who?
MAGDA: Her name's Samantha.
MARTI: Samantha? Oh my god, don't tell her.
MAGDA: I know.
MARTI: She'll kill you.

SCENE NINE

BERNADETTE *stands behind a seated* ANGELA, *brushing her hair.*

BERNADETTE: You look beautiful, do you know that?

>ANGELA *frowns.*

You do. You look radiant.

>ANGELA's *frown deepens.*

You look well. I don't know if I can remember the last time you were well. Can you?
ANGELA: I'm not sure.
BERNADETTE: Oh dear, look here, a grey hair.
ANGELA: Oh no, pull it out!

>BERNADETTE *pulls out a hair, or two.*

Ow! Show me.
BERNADETTE: I've let it fall.

>*She lets it fall.*

What I don't want is to see you come toppling down. Enjoy yourself but don't put yourself under too much stress. Promise me, you won't?
ANGELA: I won't.

BERNADETTE: You mustn't let things get too much.

ANGELA: I won't.

BERNADETTE: You've got a lot going on. Too much. I don't want you getting sick.

ANGELA: [*faint*] I won't.

BERNADETTE: There's the wedding arrangements to make, the honeymoon to organise, a place for you and Peter to live. So much for you to do.

ANGELA: Yes there is, isn't there?

> ANGELA *grows more and more overwhelmed as* BERNADETTE *speaks.*

BERNADETTE: Because I know the trust so well, how it relates to the company and the royalty streams, how the dividends and franking credits, depending on the prior year tax losses, feed back into the trust; and the various safe harbours and shelters from tax and duty consequences; the nameplate capacities, the agricultural acquisitions and downstream assets, the debt and gearing levels, and the timing to up the price on the tonnage of ore they extract. I think you can leave it to me to worry about.

ANGELA: Won't Peter need something to do?

BERNADETTE: He doesn't want to deal with any of it.

ANGELA: But he'll be my husband.

BERNADETTE: He's not equipped.

ANGELA: I suppose not.

BERNADETTE: Now that your father has passed …

ANGELA: He wasn't my—

> *A good tug on* ANGELA*'s hair pulls her up short.*

BERNADETTE: … we can forgive his indulgences, which included the wonderful life he provided for you. And I can get back on track and refocus on the vision I have to make the utmost use of our land.

ANGELA: You mean my land, don't you?

BERNADETTE: Angela, my love, don't push your luck. I mean the land that your biological father intended to put our country on the map, to bring it great wealth and make it a nation as great as any other. You and Peter won't have time to worry about any of that.

ANGELA: Why's that?

BERNADETTE: You're thirty-nine, Angela, and I don't mean to be cruel, but you're running out of time.
ANGELA: Running out of time?
BERNADETTE: Yes, my love, for children. If you and Peter are planning on a child …
ANGELA: We haven't talked about it.
BERNADETTE: Children need a great deal of attention.
ANGELA: I don't know if …

>BERNADETTE *stops brushing and looks closer at* ANGELA*'s roots.*

What? Are there more?

>*Pause.*

BERNADETTE: Not that I can see.

SCENE TEN

A hot and frustrated ADELE *roams the space. She finally stands in front of the air conditioner in an effort to cool down.*

MAGDA *and* MARTI *enter wearing lace underwear. They are childlike in their excitement as they show themselves off.*

MAGDA: Get a load of this!
MARTI: Angela bought them for us.
MAGDA: She bought some for you too, Adele.

>*They pull a pose.* ADELE *is contemptuous.*

MARTI: They're real lace.
MAGDA: Aren't they gorgeous?

>*Another pose.*

MARTI: I love nice underwear.

>*And another.*

MAGDA: I look like a bombshell.
MARTI: You do.
MAGDA: You do too.
MARTI: Why, thank you.
MAGDA: Angela's bought herself a dozen pairs.
MARTI: All colours.

MAGDA: And a beautiful negligee.
MARTI: For her wedding night.
MAGDA: Imagine her? Standing there aquiver.

> ADELE *resists imagining* ANGELA *on her wedding night with all her might.*

MARTI: Peter won't be able to keep his hands off her.
MAGDA: He'll be smothering her with kisses.
MARTI: He'll be lifting her up in his arms.
MAGDA: He'll be laying her down on the bed.
MARTI: Or on the shag pile.
MAGDA: And he'll whisper in her ear.
MARTI: Don't worry, I'll be gentle.
MAGDA: And in the next second he'll be humping the life out of her.

> ADELE *puts her hands over her ears and silently screams.*

Lucky Angela.
MARTI: Lucky, lucky Angela.

> MARIA *enters. She stares agog at* MAGDA *and* MARTI *in their underwear. She circles them.*

MARIA: [*chuckling*] That's the way. Good for you. Whatever you have to do. Bravo. Bravo. Fabulous. Fabulous. [*At* MARTI*'s breasts*] How I'd like to get my hands on them. [*At* MAGDA*'s buttocks*] Oh, and them. Fabulous. Perfect for a bit of a squeeze.

> *Staring at her granddaughters all the while and chuckling lewdly,* MARIA *makes her own way out.*

Don't worry, I'll lock the door behind me.

> *She stops.*

I didn't think you had it in you. Lovely, lovely.

> *She gestures with her hands at their breasts once more and exits.*

> ANGELA *bursts in furiously.*

ANGELA: Where's the singlet?
ADELE: What singlet?
ANGELA: It was under my pillow.
ADELE: A singlet?

MAGDA: A singlet?
ADELE: Who'd want your singlet?
ANGELA: Where's the singlet?
ADELE: What singlet?
ANGELA: One of you has stolen it.
MAGDA: Don't be ridiculous, your singlet wouldn't fit us.
ANGELA: It's Peter's.
ADELE: Peter's singlet?
ANGELA: He took it off.
MAGDA: Whoa! Angela!
ADELE: I don't believe it.
ANGELA: To change it. It was soaked in sweat.
MAGDA: Whoa! Angela!
ANGELA: He'd been working and had forgotten to change before his visit.
MARTI: You put his dirty, sweaty singlet under your pillow?
ANGELA: It was in my room and now it's gone.
MAGDA: Maybe it jumped out your window in the middle of the night.
MARTI: Peter likes to walk around in the moonlight.
ANGELA: It's not funny! I'm telling him when he comes.
MAGDA: Tell him, who gives a stuff!
ANGELA: Where is it?
MARTI: I don't know.
ADELE: Nor do I.
ANGELA: Which one of you took it?
MAGDA: We didn't take the bloody singlet.
MARTI: Don't accuse us of taking your stuff.
ANGELA: I want to know which one of you took it.
ADELE: Somebody took it. But not me!
MARTI: Of course it wouldn't be you!
MAGDA: Well, it wasn't me!

    BERNADETTE *and* PENELOPE *enter.*

BERNADETTE: Silence! What's all this shouting about? People can hear you across the state, the noise you're making.

  She does a double take at her DAUGHTERS *in their underwear.*

 Why haven't you got your clothes on?
ANGELA: They've stolen Peter's singlet.

BERNADETTE: His singlet? What are you doing with his singlet?
MAGDA: She had it under her pillow.
ANGELA: They've stolen it.
BERNADETTE: Who has?
ANGELA: They have!

>BERNADETTE *sighs.*

BERNADETTE: Which of you has it?

>*Pause.*

Answer me.

>*Pause.*

Who took the singlet? Who took the bloody singlet?! [*To* PENELOPE] Search their rooms. Look in their beds. In their drawers.

>PENELOPE *exits.*

Why cause Angela pain? I'm sick of you. [*To* ANGELA] You're sure it's missing?
ANGELA: Yes.
BERNADETTE: You looked everywhere?
ANGELA: Yes!
BERNADETTE: Peter Romano's singlet? His singlet, for Christ's sake. Leave your sister be. Why are you causing me grief like this?

>PENELOPE *enters.*

PENELOPE: Here it is!
BERNADETTE: Where was it?
PENELOPE: It was ...
BERNADETTE: Who's the culprit?
PENELOPE: [*wonderingly*] It was between the sheets in Marti's bed.
BERNADETTE: Really?

>*She turns to* MARTI.

Marti? Really?
MARTI: Yes.
BERNADETTE: What's this about? What are you upsetting Angela for? Answer me!

>*She steps forward suddenly, her arm raised.*

I'd like to give you a good slap.

MARTI: Try it.
BERNADETTE: You don't think I would? Say you're sorry.
MARTI: No! Why?
BERNADETTE: Why did you take the bloody singlet?
MARTI: It was a joke.
ADELE: It wasn't a joke! You don't even like jokes.

> ADELE *and* MARTI *whisper conspiratorially.*

There's something else going on. Admit it, Marti.
MARTI: Careful, Adele, because if I speak now then everything will be out. I'll blab my bloody head off.
ADELE: What the hell! What've you got to tell?
MAGDA: What are you two talking about?
ADELE: Marti's nasty imagination has got the better of her.
ANGELA: It's not my fault that Peter Romano chose me!

> *Pause. The* SISTERS *laugh.*

ADELE: For your trust funds.
ANGELA: Mum!
BERNADETTE: Stop!
MARTI: For your land.
ANGELA: Mum!
BERNADETTE: Stop!
MAGDA: For your property.
ANGELA: Mum!
BERNADETTE: I said stop! Can't you be together for this short time without your hatred for one another leaking out?
ADELE: Peter doesn't want Angela.
BERNADETTE: You make me sick at heart.
MAGDA: Fucking Peter Romano is going to take it all! Every bloody cent!
BERNADETTE: Out of here! Go! [*To* MARTI *and* MAGDA] And put some bloody clothes on!

> *They exit to their rooms.*

SCENE ELEVEN

PENELOPE *is back on her hands and knees wiping dust from the white tiles.*

ADELE *enters. She stands childlike, overcome by the heat.*

ADELE: I'm exhausted. It's killing me, this heat. I'm dying here.

In the far distance a siren sounds.

PENELOPE: The change of shift. The miners are going down for the evening stint.

ADELE *listens intently as it sounds again.*

ADELE: I wish I was going with them. I'd love to go down the mine. I'd love to work, I don't know, hard, with my hands, with my entire body.

PENELOPE *stops work for a moment to roll her eyes at* ADELE.

To feel strong. To sweat. To pit myself against something. It would be so satisfying.

PENELOPE: So many young men, far from their homes, working long hours in this terrible heat, I don't know.

ADELE: I want to do that.

PENELOPE: They're making money hand over fist though. There must be satisfaction in that. Not a lot of satisfaction elsewhere; they're short on women in town this season, I hear. Last week there was a line-up of thirty men, and just one girl to service them all. Imagine that, if you can.

ADELE: One woman for all those men?

PENELOPE: You'd be working your body hard then.

ADELE: Oh my god!

PENELOPE: You'd be working up a right old sweat.

ADELE: Oh my god!

PENELOPE: My mother gave my brothers money so they could go into the town and pay for a girl.

ADELE: Men get away with everything.

PENELOPE: Men need sex, that's that.

ADELE: We don't get to do anything like that.

PENELOPE: Thank Christ.

The siren sounds once more.

There they go.

ADELE: Deep down below. I wish I was one of them. I want to come and go. I want to use my body freely, to do with it whatever I please.

PENELOPE: What are you talking about, Adele?
ADELE: If we could do that then we could forget what's eating us.
PENELOPE: What's eating us?
ADELE: Each of us has something.
PENELOPE: Each of us?
ADELE: Eating away at us.

She smiles secretively but PENELOPE *catches her out.*

What?
PENELOPE: Don't even think about it.
ADELE: I don't know what you're talking about.
PENELOPE: Angela's old and sickly and on the shelf. It's not likely she'll find anyone else. You will. You've got time. Be fair, for god's sake.
ADELE: What a tremendous affection you suddenly have for my sister. I wonder why that might be.
PENELOPE: I don't have any affection for any of you. All I want is to live in peace. And I don't want to find myself out on the street.
ADELE: Mind your own business.
PENELOPE: You can't like him that much, Adele.
ADELE: But I do, I do. So much. I look into his eyes and I lose myself. Completely.
PENELOPE: I'm going to stick to you like glue.

A stand-off. PENELOPE *wins out and* ADELE *exits.*

SCENE TWELVE

BERNADETTE *and* PENELOPE *stand under the air conditioner, their faces up and their arms akimbo.*

PENELOPE: You think Peter is going to be satisfied?
BERNADETTE: What nonsense are you dragging up?
PENELOPE: Will Angela be enough for him?
BERNADETTE: Penelope, I know when you've got your knife out.
PENELOPE: I'm not trying to hurt you, Bernadette, I'm trying to warn you.
BERNADETTE: Warn me about what?
PENELOPE: You see what other people are up to a hundred kilometres away, but when it comes to your children, you're blind.

BERNADETTE: I know my children, Penelope.
PENELOPE: Why do you think Marti took his singlet?
BERNADETTE: You heard her, it was a silly joke.
PENELOPE: Marti's lovesick.
BERNADETTE: Lovesick?
PENELOPE: Why didn't you let her marry James Dalton? When you knew they loved each other?
BERNADETTE: If James Dalton loved her so much why did he let her go?
PENELOPE: Because you sent him a letter that you wrote but signed it from Marti. He believed she didn't want him.
BERNADETTE: There's no way I would allow that family anywhere near mine.
PENELOPE: She loved him! He loved her! Why did you do it? Because of some silly idea that you're better than everyone else.
BERNADETTE: I have that idea because I can afford to.
PENELOPE: Peter and Angela seem wrong to me.
BERNADETTE: She wants him and she's got him.
PENELOPE: To anyone it would seem wrong.
BERNADETTE: I can't take the risk some other ambitious buck won't make a move and take over. Peter will do as I say.
PENELOPE: Peter and Adele are a better match.
BERNADETTE: Adele? Don't be ridiculous. Where's the sense in that?
PENELOPE: Last night I woke up and heard talking at four-thirty.
BERNADETTE: Four-thirty?
PENELOPE: I heard talking, I tell you. It's Peter, and it's not with Angela, he's talking.
BERNADETTE: Not another bloody word! Do you realise what's at stake, Penelope? Do you? I'm on the brink of being exactly like you.
PENELOPE: Like me?
BERNADETTE: With nothing. And do you realise what that means, Penelope? For you?

PENELOPE does realise. She zips her mouth.

SCENE THIRTEEN

Late. The room fills with the deafening sounds of revving cars and barking dogs.

Alarmed, BERNADETTE *and her* DAUGHTERS *enter the space.*

PENELOPE *enters, bursting with news.*

PENELOPE: They're pissed. Drunk as skunks. Off their heads. Ugly. The ugliest I've seen. And mean. Dogs. On the hunt. It's Rosie they're after. They've picked up her scent. They reckon she was headed out this way.

BERNADETTE: Have you locked the doors?

PENELOPE: Of course.

BERNADETTE: Can she get in?

PENELOPE: Not a chance.

ADELE: Help her. Help her, Mum. Please.

BERNADETTE: I've got no time for girls like Rosie. Do you hear me, Adele? No time at all.

ADELE: Please, Mum.

BERNADETTE: I'll be helping no-one.

END OF ACT TWO

ACT THREE

SCENE FOURTEEN

The DAUGHTERS *are in their rooms. Like caged animals, they pace.*

The night looms around a dining table. It's as if it's marooned, cut off from the world.

BERNADETTE, PENELOPE *and* MARIA *are seated at the table.*

An insect zapper, hanging above their heads, occasionally sparks and zaps.

PENELOPE *spoonfeeds* MARIA *who disturbs the silence with her slurping.*

The DAUGHTERS *line up like prisoners, and as if on cue, together they step out of their rooms.*

They enter and seat themselves at the table.

MARIA *slurps some more.*

A sudden resounding blow brings their heads up in alarm.

They listen for it and it comes: another blow.

MAGDA: I felt that in my chest.
MARTI: I did too.
BERNADETTE: He's hot.

> MARIA *laughs lustily.*

MARIA: He's hot alright.

> *Another resounding blow.*
>
> *The* DAUGHTERS *giggle.*

BERNADETTE: Enough!

> *They stop.*
>
> *Another blow sets the* DAUGHTERS *giggling again.*

   Enough, I said.
PENELOPE: When's he being put to the cows?
BERNADETTE: At daybreak.

PENELOPE: He's a fine specimen.
BERNADETTE: He'll do the job.

The blow.

MARIA: By the sound of it, he'll do it well.

ADELE gets up from the table.

BERNADETTE: Where are you going?
ADELE: For a drink of water.
BERNADETTE: [*to* PENELOPE] Bring a pitcher of water. [*To* ADELE] You. Sit.

ADELE sits. PENELOPE fetches a pitcher of water.

Silence.

PENELOPE: [*to* ANGELA] So, the date's all set?
BERNADETTE: It's all arranged.
PENELOPE: You must be happy.
BERNADETTE: Of course she's happy.
PENELOPE: Looking forward to the big day.
BERNADETTE: Yes, yes.
PENELOPE: And the honeymoon?
BERNADETTE: Yes, yes, and the bloody honeymoon.

ADELE knocks the salt shaker over.

PENELOPE: You've spilled the salt! Throw it over your left shoulder.
MARTI: She couldn't get any more bad luck than she's having.
ADELE: Being anywhere near you feels bad luck.
BERNADETTE: That's enough!
PENELOPE: Show me your ring, Angela.

ANGELA lifts her hand for PENELOPE to see.

Beautiful. Three pearls. In my day pearls signified tears.
ANGELA: Things have changed.
ADELE: I don't think things like that change.
PENELOPE: Engagement rings are meant to be diamonds.
BERNADETTE: It's a beautiful ring.
MARTI: Can I see it?

ANGELA ignores her.

PENELOPE: Diamonds are the more usual choice.
MARTI: Let me have a look.
BERNADETTE: Pearls or diamonds, Peter's intentions are clear.
MARTI: Angela, show me your ring.
ANGELA: No, Marti, you'll probably take it and put it under your pillow.

ADELE rises.

BERNADETTE: Where are you going?
ADELE: To my room.
BERNADETTE: Sit.

She sits.

ANGELA: We've been looking at apartments. I want one by the sea but Peter wants one in the centre of the city. I've bought most of the furniture off the net and I'll wait until we're settled before I buy the rest.
MAGDA: That must have cost a pretty penny.
ANGELA: Unbelievable, so much, and then I thought, so what? I've got it, I can spend whatever I like.

Her SISTERS stare loathingly at her.

I haven't even started on the kitchen stuff or the paintings for the walls. I'll get Peter to help with that.

Silence.

Five sofas. Three Chesterfields and two Morans. Lovely, they are. For the lounge. Comfortable. Lovely. Really lovely. Great for when we have company.

Silence.

The bed's enormous. Peter insisted. King-size. And hard. Peter likes a hard bed. It's so big, Peter says he thinks I might get lost in it.

She giggles uncomfortably.

I've bought a lot of the bedding, the sheets are Arabian cotton. Beautiful. I'm sure the feel of them will be lovely. They're on order and come with matching doona cover sets. One set is hand embroidered with gorgeous peacocks with their tail feathers spread.
BERNADETTE: Angela, go easy. You know what we talked about. It's lovely for you to set up house. Lovely. But enough is enough.
ANGELA: But you said—

BERNADETTE: Go easy now. Don't forget your wedding will set you back, and the honeymoon, and all that.

ANGELA *sulks.*

ADELE *quickly rises.*

ADELE: I'm going to walk as far as the gate to stretch my legs.

She looks at her mother expecting to be denied. BERNADETTE *cues* MARTI *instead.*

MARTI: I'll join you.

MAGDA: Me too.

ADELE: I'm not going to get lost!

BERNADETTE: You should always have company at night. Snakes. No matter the time there are always snakes about.

MARIA *stands.*

MARIA: Wait for me.

BERNADETTE: Lock her up.

ADELE, MARTI *and* MAGDA *exit.*

PENELOPE *takes* MARIA *by the arm and diverts her from following them.*

MARIA *cries.*

MARIA: I want to go out. I want to go out.

PENELOPE *and* MARIA *exit.*

BERNADETTE: What time did Peter go last night?

ANGELA: Twelve-thirty.

BERNADETTE: What does he talk about?

ANGELA: He talks about working in the mine and how he can't wait for the day he can stop. Sometimes I find him so distracted. If I ask him what's the matter, he answers, 'I've got a lot on my mind'.

BERNADETTE: Don't ask him. And when you're married ask him even less because you won't get the answers you want.

ANGELA: He goes silent.

BERNADETTE: Nothing wrong with a bit of quiet.

ANGELA: For ages.

BERNADETTE: You will learn to crave the quiet. Silence is golden, they say.

ANGELA: Is this what it's meant to be like when you're in love?
BERNADETTE: Peter's young. He wants to marry you. You want to be a wife. You want a man to share your life. You've got one.
ANGELA: I never know what he's thinking.
BERNADETTE: Don't be too inquisitive. You'll find out things that you don't want to know.
ANGELA: I thought I'd be happy, but I'm not.
BERNADETTE: You're happy enough.
ANGELA: I wanted to be happy.
BERNADETTE: You're just not used to it. You're happy. Happy enough. Is he coming tonight?
ANGELA: No, he's gone to the city to see his mum.
BERNADETTE: Good. We'll go to bed early and get a good night's rest.

SCENE FIFTEEN

ADELE *emerges from darkness.*

ADELE: It's so wonderfully dark. I could disappear and nobody would find me.

    MARTI *and* MAGDA *appear.*

MARTI: I can't see two steps in front of me.
MAGDA: Anyone could sneak up behind us.
ADELE: Go back if you're afraid.
MARTI: Did you see the bull?
MAGDA: He's huge.
MARTI: He almost fills the entire corral.
MAGDA: Did you see the balls on him?
MARTI: The poor cows.
MAGDA: Thank god, he's tethered.
MARTI: Why have we come so far?
MAGDA: I can't see the lights back at the house.
ADELE: Go. Go back.
MARTI: It's dangerous out here on your own.
MAGDA: We should turn back.

    ADELE *lifts her head to the sky.*

ADELE: Look at those stars. They're as big as fists.

    MARTI *looks up.*

MARTI: You get a crick in your neck doing this.
ADELE: Look at them, would you?
MAGDA: I couldn't give two shits about what goes on over the roof.
ADELE: Oh, Magda, look.
MAGDA: I have trouble enough with what happens under it.
ADELE: I'm going to stay out here until I see one fall.
MARTI: It'll be a bad omen if you do.
ADELE: Something that has been quiet for years and years, quietly waiting, and then suddenly running like fire across the sky. How wonderful is that?
MAGDA: Come on, let's go.
MARTI: Adele, come on.
ADELE: It's a beautiful night. The sky and the stars remind me how magnificent the world is.
MARTI: It's overwhelming is what it is.
MAGDA: It's fucking dark.
ADELE: Would you please both go away?
MAGDA: Don't step on any snakes.
ADELE: Go inside. Leave me be.
MARTI: No way.
MAGDA: It's time to go in.
ADELE: You go in!
MARTI: We're not leaving you out here alone.
MAGDA: Anything could happen to you.
ADELE: I want it to!

    BERNADETTE *calls from the darkness.*

BERNADETTE: Girls! Girls!
ADELE: Shit! Why can't you leave me alone?

    They go inside.

SCENE SIXTEEN

BERNADETTE *stands in semi-darkness, listening, super-vigilant, on guard.*

MAGDA *enters and* BERNADETTE *turns on her like a cat about to pounce.*

MAGDA: Where am I?

BERNADETTE: Where are you?
MAGDA: Where do I stand?
BERNADETTE: I don't know.
MAGDA: What am I going to do?
BERNADETTE: That's entirely up to you.
MAGDA: I thought you'd have a plan.
BERNADETTE: I imagined that when the eight weeks is up you'll make a beeline back to the city.
MAGDA: How am I going to live?
BERNADETTE: Perhaps the flatmate has kept your room.
MAGDA: She's not my flatmate.
BERNADETTE: I know.
MAGDA: She's my—
BERNADETTE: —girlfriend. I know.
MAGDA: I didn't mean to keep it from you.
BERNADETTE: I gather no-one else knows.
MAGDA: Marti knows. No-one else.
BERNADETTE: I agree with you. Less said …
MAGDA: What?
BERNADETTE: … the better.
MAGDA: No.
BERNADETTE: Why make a big deal about these things when they're over.
MAGDA: It's not over.
BERNADETTE: You've always been a dabbler. You never kept at a hobby. Angela had her stamps, Marti liked to sew, Adele was horse mad, you tried a few things but just for a while was more your style.
MAGDA: This is not just for a while. I've been with Samantha for a couple of years.
BERNADETTE: You've been in a relationship for years that no-one knows anything about.
MAGDA: Mum, I'm serious about Samantha.
BERNADETTE: You've never been serious about anything in your life.
MAGDA: I'm serious now.
BERNADETTE: You've started at least half a dozen university courses. Wanted to be a lawyer, a biologist, a social worker. At some point there was even talk of you being a nurse. How long did you last with your business degree?

MAGDA: I was about to re-enrol when Dad got ill.
BERNADETTE: Of all my children, I thought that you showed the most promise, you had some nous, I thought. You might follow in my footsteps but no, you too, so easily distracted.
MAGDA: I can restart my course immediately.
BERNADETTE: Too easily swayed.
MAGDA: I'm ready to put my head down.
BERNADETTE: You'll lose direction the moment you're away.
MAGDA: Give me a chance. Let me help with the business.
BERNADETTE: You'd need to stay. Here. And work. With me.

> *Pause.*

Got the metal? Or will another Samantha come along and take your attention?
MAGDA: I love Samantha.
BERNADETTE: Well, you go, you go to her, Magda. Take the bull by the horns and go.
MAGDA: I will.
BERNADETTE: If you choose to live on the edge, you're on your own.

> *Pause.*

MAGDA: Okay. Fine.
BERNADETTE: Good.

> *Pause.*

MAGDA: No, perfectly fine.
BERNADETTE: Oh, good.

> *Pause.*

MAGDA: I might need a bit of help for a little while?
BERNADETTE: No.
MAGDA: No. Okay.

> *Pause.*

Until I get back on my feet.
BERNADETTE: No.
MAGDA: You're right. I'll manage.
BERNADETTE: Of course you will.

> MAGDA *exits.*

SCENE SEVENTEEN

Darkness. A determined knocking.
PENELOPE *enters.* BERNADETTE *sits, hyper-vigilant at the table.*

BERNADETTE: Tell her she has to go.
PENELOPE: I've told her.
BERNADETTE: Tell her again.
PENELOPE: She's determined.
BERNADETTE: What's she want, that's what I'd like to know?
PENELOPE: Same old same old.
BERNADETTE: Give her some money and tell her to be on her way.
PENELOPE: Tried that.
BERNADETTE: Offer her a bit more.
PENELOPE: She doesn't want it, she says.
BERNADETTE: Rubbish. She's waiting to take us to the cleaners, that's all.
PENELOPE: She's never taken it before.
BERNADETTE: Rosie, Rosie, Rosie, this is too much.

More knocking.

She'll wake the girls.
PENELOPE: I'll see if I can move her on.
BERNADETTE: I'll beat her with a stick if you can't shift her.

PENELOPE *exits. The knocking ceases.*

Rosie, Rosie, Rosie, enough's enough.

PENELOPE *enters.*

You're rid of her?
PENELOPE: For now. I told her to come back tomorrow.
BERNADETTE: Oh no.
PENELOPE: And I'd show her her father's ashes.
BERNADETTE: Keep your voice down. Tony's dead, for god's sake. Dead. There's no claim she can make. This land is mine. Mine, for god's sake.
PENELOPE: He was her father. She wants it acknowledged, that's all.
BERNADETTE: Yes, sure sure sure.
PENELOPE: I really do think that's all.

BERNADETTE: Do not say another word.

She turns suddenly to see her DAUGHTERS *have collected at the door.*

Back to bed. Now. There's nothing to worry about.

PENELOPE *and* BERNADETTE *listen to the night.*

PENELOPE: Can you hear the silence, the terrible silence in this house?
BERNADETTE: I can.
PENELOPE: I'm frightened, Bernadette. I don't know exactly why. I feel so terribly frightened.
BERNADETTE: Angela will be married soon and then everything will be fine. Life will go on as usual. We will be safe, you and I.
PENELOPE: You can't stop what's going on inside.
BERNADETTE: If whatever is going on inside stays inside, I don't mind.
PENELOPE: Something terrible is on its way, but you don't want to listen to a word I say.

They exit.

SCENE EIGHTEEN

Dogs howl outside.

PENELOPE *peers out into the darkness.*

PENELOPE: What's out there disturbing the dogs?

ADELE *enters, wearing a white petticoat. Furtive.*

Why aren't you in bed?
ADELE: I'm thirsty.

She drinks from a glass on the table.

PENELOPE: You should be asleep.
ADELE: I woke up because I needed a drink. Why don't you go to bed?
PENELOPE: I will. In a while.

PENELOPE *waits stubbornly until* ADELE *exits.*

The dogs howl some more.

Don't know how any of us will get to sleep tonight.

PENELOPE *exits.*

MARIA *enters. She carries a lamb in her arms.*

MARIA: [*singing*]
> Rock-a-bye baby
> In the tree top
> When the wind blows
> The cradle will rock
> When the bough breaks
> The cradle will fall
> And down will come baby
> Cradle and all.

ADELE *enters. She looks about cautiously, and quietly, not to alert her grandmother, disappears out into the night.*

MARTI *enters. She's looking for* ADELE *and finds* MARIA *instead.*

MARTI: Grandma, what are you doing?
MARIA: Will you open the door for me? Who are you?
MARTI: How did you get out?
MARIA: I escaped.
MARTI: Go back to bed.
MARIA: You're Marti. Now, I see you. Marti, face of a martyr. When are you going to have a baby? I've had this one.
MARTI: Where did you get that lamb?
MARIA: I know it's a lamb. But can't a lamb be a baby? It's better to have a lamb than not have anything at all. [*Calling out*] Hey, old Bernadette, leopard face!
MARTI: Don't shout.
MARIA: Just because I have white hair you think I can't have babies, but I can—babies and babies and babies. This baby will have white hair and I'll have this baby, and another, and then one other; and we'll be like the waves—one, then another, and another. All of us will have white heads. We'll be sea foam. There's no sea foam here. Nothing but mourning shrouds here.
MARTI: Shush, Grandma, shush.
MARIA: When my neighbour had a baby, I'd take her some chocolate and later she'd bring me some, and so on—always and always and always. You'll have white hair but your neighbours won't come. I have to go away, but I'm afraid the dogs will bite me. I don't like the

desert. I like houses, but open houses where the neighbour women sleep in their beds with their little tots, and the men outside sit in their chairs. Peter Romano is a giant. All of you love him. But he's going to devour you because you're chaff. No, not chaff. Frogs with no tongues!

MARTI: [*pushing her angrily*] Off to bed.

MARIA: You'll open the door for me, won't you?

MARTI: Yes, yes, I will.

MARTI escorts MARIA out.

MARIA: [*weeping*] Rock-a-bye baby
      In the tree top
      When the wind blows
      The cradle will rock ...

A last pitiful cry from MARIA from within the house.

I want to go out.

SCENE NINETEEN

MARTI *stands outside in the darkness. The stars offer the only light.*

MARTI: Adele!

She tentatively steps further out into the dark.

Adele!

ADELE *emerges from the dark.*

ADELE: Keep your voice down.

MARTI: Keep away from him.

ADELE: Don't tell me what to do.

MARTI: You pushed yourself on him.

ADELE: He's always wanted me.

MARTI: I'm not going to let you snatch him from Angela.

ADELE: You know better than me that he doesn't love her.

MARTI: Yes, I know.

ADELE: You know because you know he loves me. Me!

MARTI: Shut up, Adele! I don't want to hear it.

ADELE: He can be with Angela for a hundred years, but the idea of him having his arms around me seems terrible to you.

MARTI: It tears me apart. I hurt. Here. I hurt, as if my chest is about to burst.
ADELE: [*impulsively hugging her*] Marti, Marti, it's not my fault!
MARTI: Don't put your arms around me! This isn't something that can be smoothed over. I don't feel a sister to you.

She pushes ADELE *away.*

ADELE: There's no going back for me. I have had his skin against mine, I have the taste of him in my mouth.
MARTI: Be quiet!
ADELE: I love him, Marti, I love him so much.
MARTI: I said, be quiet.
ADELE: I'll wear the crown of tumbleweed in my hair, be pointed at, face the sneers, be the mistress of the man married to my sister.
MARTI: Shut up, Adele.
ADELE: Let him marry Angela. I'll have my own place and he'll come to me whenever he wants.

A whistle sounds. ADELE *turns.* MARTI *blocks her.*

MARTI: Where do you think you're going?
ADELE: Get out of my way.
MARTI: Pass me if you can.
ADELE: Get out of my way!
MARTI: [*shouting*] Mum! Mum!
ADELE: Let me go!
MARTI: Mum!

BERNADETTE *emerges from the darkness.*

BERNADETTE: What's going on?
MARTI: She's going to Peter.
BERNADETTE: What have you done, Adele?
ADELE: I belong with Peter and that's where I'm going.

MAGDA, PENELOPE *and* ANGELA *emerge.*

MARTI: Guess who's been with your boyfriend, Angela?
ADELE: We're in love. We're going to be together. He's waiting for me.
BERNADETTE: Adele, you have made such a mistake.
ADELE: How can two people loving each other be a mistake?
BERNADETTE: Love has nothing to do with it.

ADELE: I'm going to him.

> MARTI *stands in her way.*

MARTI: There's no way I'll let you pass.
BERNADETTE: I will speak to Peter. Alone. He can choose to be with you, Adele, or to marry Angela. One, or the other.

> *She exits.*
>
> *In silence, they wait.* ADELE *holds herself high, confident she will be with Peter.*
>
> BERNADETTE *returns.*

Angela, the arrangements will continue as planned.
ANGELA: I don't want him if he—
BERNADETTE: The arrangement will continue as planned.
ADELE: Where is he?
BERNADETTE: Gone.
ADELE: I don't believe you.
BERNADETTE: All done. All through. Over, it's over, Adele. Over. Back to boarding school for you. The next time you will see him is at Angela's wedding.

> ADELE *tries to run to Peter but she is blocked by each of her* SISTERS. *Finally, she turns and retreats quickly inside.*

ANGELA: Did he really choose me?
BERNADETTE: He saw me and took to his heels. I've never seen a man run so fast.
ANGELA: You don't know what choice he'd make.
BERNADETTE: I've chosen for him.

> *Silence.*

SCENE TWENTY

BERNADETTE *stands in the centre of the room.*

Adele's room is dark.

PENELOPE *and the* DAUGHTERS *call for her.*

PENELOPE: Adele! Adele! Adele, open the door.
MAGDA: Open up, Adele.

MARTI: Adele?
ANGELA: Open the door.
PENELOPE: She won't answer.
MARTI: Adele! Open up!
ANGELA: Don't be ridiculous, Adele.
MAGDA: Open the fucking door!
PENELOPE: She's not going to open it.
ANGELA: For Christ's sake, Adele, open the door!
PENELOPE: Adele, open the door.
MAGDA: Adele!
MARTI: Adele!
ANGELA: Adele!

Silence. All the while BERNADETTE *waits.*

BERNADETTE: Push against the door.

PENELOPE and the DAUGHTERS disappear in the darkness of Adele's room.

Silence. Terrible silence. BERNADETTE *knows.*

Nothing is to be said of this. And no crying. Tears when you're alone. We'll drown ourselves in a sea of mourning. But for now, nothing is to be said about the cause of our sadness. Silence. Do you hear me? Silence, I said.

Silence.

THE END

www.currency.com.au

Visit Currency Press' website now to:
- Buy your books online
- Browse through our full list of titles, from plays to screenplays, books on theatre, film and music, and more
- Choose a play for your school or amateur performance group by cast size and gender
- Obtain information about performance rights
- Find out about theatre productions and other performing arts news across Australia
- For students, read our study guides
- For teachers, access syllabus and other relevant information
- Sign up for our email newsletter

The performing arts publisher

www.ingramcontent.com/pod-product-compliance
Lightning Source LLC
Chambersburg PA
CBHW040306170426
43194CB00022B/2914